Attitudes to flexible working and family life

Diane M. Houston and Julie A. Waumsley

First published in Great Britain in December 2003 by

The Policy Press
Fourth Floor, Beacon House
Queen's Road
Bristol BS8 1QU
UK

Tel no +44 (0)117 331 4054
Fax no +44 (0)117 331 4093
E-mail tpp-info@bristol.ac.uk
www.policypress.org.uk

Reprinted 2004

Published for the Joseph Rowntree Foundation by The Policy Press

ISBN 1 86134 549 6

British Library Cataloguing in Publication Data
A catalogue record for this report is available from the British Library.

Library of Congress Cataloging-in-Publication Data
A catalog record for this report has been requested.

Diane M. Houston is a Senior Lecturer in Psychology at the University of Kent, where she directs the Work–Life Research Group. **Julie A. Waumsley** was the Research Associate on this project and is a member of the Work–Life Research Group.

The **Joseph Rowntree Foundation** has supported this project as part of its programme of research and innovative development projects, which it hopes will be of value to policy makers, practitioners and service users. The facts presented and views expressed in this report are, however, those of the authors and not necessarily those of the Foundation.

The statements and opinions contained within this publication are solely those of the authors and not of The University of Bristol or The Policy Press. The University of Bristol and The Policy Press disclaim responsibility for any injury to persons or property resulting from any material published in this publication.

The Policy Press works to counter discrimination on grounds of gender, race, disability, age and sexuality.

Cover design by Qube Design Associates, Bristol
Printed in Great Britain by Hobbs the Printers Ltd, Southampton

Contents

Acknowledgements

The authors would like to thank the Joseph Rowntree Foundation for sponsorship of this research. The project was supported by an advisory group and we thank members of this for their input and comments: Tom Beardshaw, David Coates, Ulrike Hotopp, John Lloyd, Joy MacMillan, Kate Purcell and Joanna Wade. We are also very grateful to John Lloyd and Katherine Lloyd for enabling us to conduct the research with members of the Amalgamated Engineering and Electrical Union. Gillian Marks, Lizanne Allcock and Nic McKenzie also made valuable contributions at various stages of the research. Particular thanks go to Shirley Dex and Barbara Ballard for their support and comments on previous drafts.

The first author's own attitudes to flexible working and family life were also transformed during this project, the analysis and writing phase coinciding with the birth of twins. Their transformation into thriving healthy girls is a much greater miracle than getting this report to press.

Introduction

On 9 March 2000 Tony Blair launched the government's campaign to promote a better work–life balance at a business breakfast at 10 Downing Street. The campaign aims to encourage employers to introduce flexible working practices and has three key elements: the setting up of Employers for Work–Life Balance, a group of 22 employers who are committed to promoting good practice; the publication of *Changing patterns in a changing world*, a Department for Education and Employment discussion document; and the Challenge Fund, launched in June 2000, a financial resource to help employers to develop and implement work–life balance strategies.

Until recently the government's approach was limited to positive encouragement and facilitation of companies who sought to create greater work–life balance for their workforce. However, since 6 April 2003, parents with children aged under six, or disabled children aged under 18, have the right to request a flexible working pattern and their employers have a duty to consider their applications seriously – hence there is now a legislative measure against which the impact and uptake of flexible working may be judged.

The current promotion of work–life balance issues reflects changes in the economic and political climate as well as social changes. The drive for change in employment practices is, to some extent, related to the needs of employees. Increasingly few families now reflect the traditional model of fathers who work and mothers who remain at home to care for children. In many families both partners work, and there are many families run by lone parents. This change has highlighted the need for both men and women to strike a balance between home and work in order to be effective workers, carers and parents, as well as to maintain their psychological and physical health. However, the drive for change is also related to the needs of employers. Within business, changes in customer demands and expectations for access to goods and services 24 hours a day means that organisations must operate outside the traditional nine-to-five structure. This results in organisations having to employ people who are prepared to work flexibly outside traditional working hours. Thus, while employees need flexibility from their employers, employers demand increasing flexibility from their employees.

The concept of work–life balance and flexible working is not new. Some organisations have promoted flexible working policies over the last 20 years. However, the take-up and expansion of their policies have been slow. Often such practices have only been available to women, or only used by women. The recent government initiative attempts to promote work–life balance as an issue for all.

There are clear reasons why work–life balance policies should succeed. From the employer's perspective there are strong financial incentives in retaining trained and valued employees. The costs to employers of stress-related absence, sick leave, recruitment and retraining may considerably outweigh those involved in creating a more positive and flexible working environment. From a societal perspective there are clear costs imposed and borne by those excluded from work due to caring responsibilities, as well as the documented strain on families caused by conflicts between work and home (Dex, 1999).

International research shows that government support for work–life balance and family-friendly policies is not a sufficient condition for their implementation or uptake. Nordic countries, such as Sweden and Norway, introduced progressive policies on work and childcare in the 1970s. A year of paid parental leave was introduced which, with the exception of a few weeks around the birth, could be taken by either parent. While this enhanced the experiences of women who combine work with motherhood, it did not result in parental leave being divided equally between men and women. By the early 1990s, women were still using over 90% of the allotted days (Sandqvist, 1992). It was not until a 'daddy quota' was introduced in the late 1990s – a four-week period that could only be taken by the father – that the majority of fathers took the opportunity to use this time (Brandth and Kvande, 2001). In Sweden, since 1979, all parents of children under eight have had the right to a reduced (six-hour) day; however, it is women rather than men who use this right. Women in Sweden and Norway continue to take most of the parental leave and continue to perform most of the domestic work (Sandqvist, 1992; Statistics Norway, 2001). Further cross-cultural evidence that employees are reluctant to use family-friendly opportunities comes from the US. A study of 80 major American employers found that less than 2% of their employees made use of work–family programmes (Galinsky et al, 1993). Another study, of engineers, found that employees were reluctant to take advantage of work–family benefits because of fear of damage to career prospects (Perlow, 1995).

The reasons why flexible employment may not succeed are based in the attitudes of both employers and employees. The common pattern of family employment in the UK is one of fathers who work long hours and mothers who work in low-paid, part-time jobs (Dex, 1999). Unless men begin to accept and use the family-friendly benefits, it is likely that current gender divisions in work will be amplified. This would further create a gender-differentiated workforce of women who need flexibility and make use of family-friendly policies and men who provide employers with flexibility, rejecting working practices that they fear may undermine their opportunities for advancement and promotion.

The overall aim of the research described in this report was to examine and compare attitudes to, and uptake of, flexible working practices by women and men, those who do and do not have caring responsibilities and those of different occupational levels. The research examined the ways in which workplace culture and individual circumstances determine attitudes to, and uptake of, flexible working practices. Perceptions of the career implications of flexible working were also explored. A model of orientation to work and personal life is proposed.

This report describes findings from this research which was conducted between 2001 and 2002. The methodology is described in detail in Chapter 2. The report is based on multivariate statistical analyses of quantitative data and includes concepts from psychological research. We have strived to achieve a balance between accessibility to the non-specialist and the need for technical content to illustrate the analyses. In order to enable the non-specialist to keep track of the findings we have put a great deal of the statistical material in Appendix A and made use of explanatory diagrams and chapter summaries.

Research methods

Key questions for this research

The key questions investigated by this research project were:

- What types of employment rights and benefits do workers prefer?
- What do shop stewards understand by the term 'flexible working' and how do they feel about family-friendly working arrangements?
- Do attitudes to flexible working arrangements differ as a function of gender, caring responsibilities and occupational level?
- Does use of, and intention to use, flexible working arrangements differ as a function of gender, caring responsibilities and occupational level?
- Is the use of flexible working arrangements linked to lower levels of stress, sickness leave and conflict between work and family?
- Does use of flexible working arrangements lead to higher levels of employee engagement?
- What is the relationship between flexible working and promotion and career prospects?
- What types of workplace culture facilitate the use of flexible working practices?
- Can we use the findings from this research to propose a model of orientation to work and family life?

The ways in which this research was carried out

The two stages of this research were conducted between 2001 and 2002. The first was a questionnaire survey of male and female managerial, skilled and semi-skilled workers, and was conducted through the Amalgamated Engineering and Electrical Union (AEEU). Until its merger with the Manufacturing, Science and Finance Union (MSF),[1] the AEEU was the UK's largest manufacturing union with over 730,000 members in the public and private sector, including 40,000 professional or managerial workers. This resulted in a large variety of organisations being represented, most of which had a predominantly male workforce. Data analysis provides comparisons between men and women, between those with and without caring responsibilities and between those at different occupational levels – managerial, skilled and semi-skilled workers.

The second part of the research was conducted through semi-structured interviews with 43 shop stewards. The interviews were held at the AEEU's residential training colleges at Cudham Hall in Kent, and Esher Place in Surrey, where the AEEU holds training courses for over 1,000 members each year. The interviews took place after training sessions, and ranged from 25 to 45 minutes in length.

The questionnaire study

The way the questionnaire survey was conducted

Ten thousand questionnaires were sent out in envelopes to the home addresses of members of the AEEU. These addresses were obtained with the cooperation of the AEEU. Our aim was to obtain a representative sample of 500 managerial,

---

[1]   After the present research began, the AEEU began a merger with MSF to become Amicus. The merger was conducted in a number of stages and the process was completed in the summer of 2003.

500 skilled and 500 semi-skilled workers. The AEEU provided a gender-balanced but otherwise random sample of their membership. A covering letter provided an outline of the research, and asked the recipient to complete the questionnaire and return it in the pre-paid envelope provided. A £200 prize draw was offered to all those who chose to also complete a prize draw card and return that with their questionnaire. It was explained that all responses were anonymous and confidential.

Response rates and sample

Just over 2,000 of the 10,000 questionnaires were returned, a 20% response rate overall. From these, 1,972 adequately completed questionnaires were coded for initial analysis.

A small number of these respondents worked part-time and a further small number had been on long-term sick leave for all or most of the previous year. These were excluded from further analysis. There were not sufficient part-time workers (61) to enable meaningful comparisons between part-time workers and full-time workers, and those on long-term sick leave had not worked for such a long period that assessment of work–life issues would have been from past rather than present experience. This left a maximum of 1,747 questionnaires for data analysis. The breakdown of male and female employees within the working categories of managerial, skilled and semi-skilled in the sample is shown in Table 2.1.[2]

The participants

The majority of respondents were white and aged between 30 and 60 years old. Most lived

Table 2.1: Breakdown of managerial, skilled and semi-skilled workers

Gender	Managerial	Skilled	Semi-skilled	Total
Male	414	579	127	1,120
Female	136	237	231	604
Total	550	816	358	1,724

[2] Men and women are not distributed evenly across occupational levels. X^2 (2df) = 175.3, $p<0.001$.

with a spouse or partner, and 37% had children under the age of 18 years. Thirty-nine per cent reported that they had some form of caring responsibilities. A breakdown of age, ethnicity, living circumstances and caring responsibilities is shown in Table 2.2.

The questionnaire

The questionnaire was designed to measure different aspects of work, personal life and work–life balance. When working practices were under investigation, these were consistently referred to as 'flexible' working rather than 'family-friendly' working. This is consistent with the ways in which these working arrangements are being represented by policy makers and also because we were interested in comparing the

Table 2.2: Breakdown of age, ethnicity, living circumstances and caring responsibilities

Sociodemographic variable	%
Age	
16–25	6
26–40	40
41–50	30
51–64	24
Ethnicity	
White	96.7
Black African	0.3
Indian	0.9
Bangladeshi	0.1
Asian	0.4
Pakistani	0.1
Chinese	0.2
Other	1.4
Living circumstances	
Alone	11.1
With spouse/partner	77.4
With parents	6.2
With friends	1.1
With your children	33.4
With your partner's children	4.0
With other relatives	0.9
Caring responsibilities	
Childcare	27.6
Care for disabled people	1.7
Care for older people	9.7
Childcare	
Children under 5 years	11.3
Children under 11 years	11.9
Children under 18 years	13.8

views of carers with non-carers. It was clear from previous research (Lloyd, 2000) and from our interviews that many people are not clear about what flexible working means. Therefore, for this section of the questionnaire, we included a definition of flexible working before the questions which asked respondents to evaluate it. This definition read as follows:

The next set of questions are about flexible working – flexible working patterns cover a wide range of options which are designed to help people combine paid work with family life or personal interests. They include part-time work, job sharing, flexitime, evening, weekend and home working. We would like to know your general views about flexible working.

In some cases items were analysed individually. In others, answers to sets of items were averaged to form a scale, either on the basis of procedures used in previous research or because the set of items was designed to measure a single construct. The items used are described below.

For most items, and unless stated otherwise, respondents simply had to indicate how much they agreed or disagreed using a 7-point Likert scale (1 = strongly disagree, 7 = strongly agree).

The questionnaire also asked respondents to report both the number of days they had taken off in sick leave during the past 12 months and the number of hours they had worked in the previous week. Also included was a section on personal and employment details.

The scales used in the questionnaire are listed below. Appendix A2.1 lists means and other statistical details for each scale. The wording in italics represents the way in which each scale or item is referred to throughout the report.

Current use of flexible working

- I already use flexible working practices.

Intention to use flexible working

- If they become available to me, I will use flexible working practices.
- I would never use flexible working practices, even if they were available to me.

Attitudes to flexible working (seven scales)

1. Personal benefits
- Flexible working arrangements are beneficial to employees.
- Flexible working practices enable people to meet family responsibilities.

2. Employer benefits
- Flexible working arrangements are beneficial to employers.

3. Employee success
- People who use flexible working practices are likely to be promoted.
- People who use flexible working practices are respected by their managers.
- People who use flexible working practices are respected by their co-workers.

4. Engagement
- People who use flexible working practices are absent less.
- People who use flexible working practices stay with the organisation longer.

5. Poor performance
- Flexible working practices lead to poor work performance.
- People who use flexible working arrangements create strain for colleagues.
- People who use flexible working practices lack motivation.

6. Long hours positive
- People who work long hours are successful.
- People who work long hours are good colleagues.

7. Long hours negative
- People who work long hours put strain on their family life.
- People who work long hours are error prone.

Conflicts in work and family life (two scales) (Netemeyer et al, 1996)

1. Work–family conflict
- The demands of my work interfere with my home and family life.
- Things I want to do at home do not get done because of the demands of my job.

- My job produces strain that makes it difficult to fulfil family demands.
- Due to work I have to make changes to my plans for family activities.
- The amount of time my job takes up makes it difficult to fulfil family responsibilities.

2. *Family–work conflict*

- My home life interferes with my responsibilities at work.
- The demands of my family or partner interfere with work-related duties.
- Family-related strain interferes with my ability to perform work-related duties.
- I have to put off doing things at work because of demands on my time at home.
- Things I want to do at work do not get done because of the demands of my family or partner.

Work–family culture in the workplace (three scales) (Thompson et al, 1999)

1. *Managerial support*

- In this organisation, employees can easily balance their work and family lives.
- In the event of a conflict, managers understand when employees have to put their family first.
- In this organisation, it is generally okay to talk about one's family at work.
- Management in this organisation encourages supervisors to be sensitive to employees' family and personal concerns.
- In general, managers in this organisation are quite accommodating of family-related needs.
- In this organisation it is very hard to leave during the working day to take care of personal or family matters.
- This organisation encourages employees to set limits on where work stops and home life begins.
- Managers in this organisation are sympathetic toward employees' childcare responsibilities.
- This organisation is supportive of employees who want to switch to less demanding jobs for family reasons.
- Managers in this organisation are sympathetic toward employees' responsibilities for the care of older people.
- In this organisation, employees are encouraged to strike a balance between their work and family lives.

2. *Negative career consequences* **of flexible working**

- To turn down a promotion or transfer for family-related reasons will seriously damage career progress in this organisation.
- Many employees are resentful when men in this organisation take extended leave to care for newborn or adopted children.
- In this organisation employees who use work–family programmes (for example, job share, part-time work) are viewed as less serious about their careers than those who do not.
- Many employees are resentful when women in this organisation take extended leave to care for newborn or adopted children.
- In this organisation employees who use flexible working are less likely to advance their career than those who do not.

3. *Organisational time demands*

- Employees are often expected to take work home at night and/or on weekends.
- Employees are regularly expected to put their jobs before their families.
- To get ahead in this organisation, employees are expected to work more than 48 hours a week.
- To be viewed favourably by management, employees in this organisation must constantly put their jobs ahead of their families or personal lives.

Family–work support

- Spending time with my family improves my performance at work.
- My family helps reduce the stress I feel at work.
- My family help me to carry out work-related duties.
- My spouse/partner plays an important role in my success at work.
- My spouse/partner provides me with practical support, which helps me at work.
- My spouse/partner provides me with emotional support, which helps me at work.

Union support for family issues

- My shop steward is sympathetic towards family-related needs.
- The AEEU is supportive of family-friendly policies.
- The AEEU is trying to implement policies that will help work–life balance.

- My union helps to protect the line between work and home.

Preferences for work and family life

- Mother looks after home and children, father works full-time.
- Father looks after home and children, mother works full-time.
- Both parents work full-time.
- Both parents use flexible working, share childcare and duties in the home.
- Mother works part-time, father works full-time.
- Father works part-time, mother works full-time.

Stress (General Health Questionnaire [GHQ]; Goldberg and Hillier, 1979)

- Have you recently been able to concentrate on whatever you're doing?
- Have you recently lost much sleep over worry?
- Have you recently felt that you are playing a useful part in things?
- Have you recently felt capable of making decisions about things?
- Have you recently felt constantly under strain?
- Have you recently felt you couldn't overcome your difficulties?
- Have you recently been able to enjoy your normal day-to-day activities?
- Have you recently been able to face up to your problems?
- Have you recently been feeling unhappy and depressed?
- Have you recently been losing confidence in yourself?
- Have you recently been thinking of yourself as a worthless person?
- Have you recently been feeling reasonably happy, all things considered?

Turnover intention (Abrams et al, 1998)

- In the next few years, I intend to leave this organisation.
- I think about leaving this organisation.
- I would like to work in this organisation until I reach retirement age.

Demographic variables

- Marital status.
- Number and ages of children.

- Caring responsibilities for people other than children.
- Job title.
- Days of sickness in the last 12 months.
- Hours worked per week.

Employment rights and benefits

Respondents were asked to rate a list of 28 employment rights and benefits, ranging from statutory maternity leave to retail vouchers. For each, respondents were asked to 'take all things into consideration' and rate how positively they felt about each (Appendix A4.1).

Statistical analysis

For multiple item scales, reliability and factor analyses were conducted to confirm that the measures were unidimensional and reliable for further analysis. Negatively worded items were reversed where necessary. Findings reported from the survey data are derived from univariate and multivariate analyses. The analyses proceeded in two stages. First, we examined mean differences in responses that could be attributed to gender differences, occupational level differences and differences in caring responsibilities (Chapters 4-8). Generally these analyses involved multivariate analysis of variance, or chi square tests. Second, we examined the relationship between the measures, using analysis multiple regression (see Chapters 5-8).

The interview study

The way the interview study was conducted

The interviews were arranged to take place on specific dates at shop steward training courses. One set of interviews took place during a morning; the remainder were held in the evenings, after dinner. The interviewer was initially introduced to the group of (predominantly male) shop stewards and explained the purpose of the research. The shop stewards were then asked to volunteer to be interviewed. Those who agreed were asked to attend the interviewing room in the order allocated. Each interview was recorded, and each interviewee was asked to complete a consent form and give some brief personal details. The interviews were semi-structured and ranged from 25 to 45 minutes in length.

During the course of the visits, 78 shop stewards were asked if they would like to take part in the interviews. Fifty-one agreed, a response rate of 65%. Interviews were conducted with 43 shop stewards; this was a smaller number than had volunteered as time constraints sometimes resulted in it being too late to conduct the final interviews of the evening. The order in which shop stewards were asked to attend for interview was based on a random counting of heads of those who volunteered. Only two women attended any of the courses at which we sought volunteers; both volunteered and were interviewed.

The interviewees

Forty-one male and two female shop stewards were interviewed. Ages ranged from 26 to 60 years, with an average age of 43 years. All except four of the interviewees lived with a spouse or partner. A third of those interviewed said that they had some form of caring responsibilities. Fifty-three per cent had a spouse or partner who worked full-time; 19% had a spouse or partner who worked part-time; 28% had a spouse or partner who did not work.

Questions asked

The topics covered in the interview included:

- Tell me a bit about the job and what it involves.
- How did you come to be a shop steward?
- How do your job role and your union role mix/combine/contrast?
- How do you feel your working life affects your personal/family life?
- What percentage of the workforce belong to (a) AEEU; (b) unions in general?
- How do you feel your family life affects your working life?
- What do you understand by the term *flexible working*?
- What do you understand by the term *work–life balance*?
- What does flexible working mean for overtime?

- What do you personally feel the pros and cons of flexible working might be?
- Are flexible working arrangements promoted in your organisation?
- In your organisation are they aimed at particular groups of people?
- What do you feel is the management attitude toward flexible working?
- Are there people in your organisation who would like greater flexibility?
- Has the AEEU been exerting pressure to introduce flexible working in the future?
- Does the AEEU promote flexible working arrangements?
- Do you prefer the term *flexible* or *family-friendly* working?

What is flexible working?

Flexible working can refer to employment flexibility in the length of time an employee works, where they carry out this work, when they work, and periods of leave that may be taken from work. The term 'family-friendly' working is also used. Often flexible working is intended to enable employees to meet the demands of both work and family responsibilities, but the same working practices can be used to enable those without family responsibilities to combine work and other aspects of life outside work.

The *Work–life balance 2000* employer survey (Hogarth et al, 2000) found that one in eight employers had no awareness of maternity leave regulations and that 76% had never heard of the government's Work–Life Balance Initiative. Other studies have also shown that employees are often unaware of flexible working options that are available to them. For example, Yeandle et al (2002) found that the majority of employees in a variety of sectors did not know about the options provided by their employers for those with caring responsibilities.

Purcell et al (1999) concluded that flexible employment means very different things for different occupational groups. Purcell et al examined contract flexibility. They found that contract flexibility did facilitate labour market participation for certain groups, such as students combining work with study. However, for many, flexible working resulted in greater job insecurity, with many flexible contracts involving poor terms and conditions of employment. At both professional and unskilled levels many flexible working contracts were found to be far from family-friendly and resulted in workers

having to extend their working hours without any notice.

This chapter reports findings from the interview study with shop stewards, described in Chapter 2. Shop stewards from the AEEU were asked to explain what they understood by the term 'flexible working' and for their views about whether such working arrangements should be called 'flexible' or 'family-friendly'. The shop stewards were also asked to give personal reflections on their own work–life balance and to give their views on what effect flexible working has/would have for their organisation.

Definitions of flexible working

The majority of shop stewards, 34 out of 43, had some understanding of what flexible working was. A typical explanation was as follows:

> "Flexible working to me is where if you have got problems at home, or got to look after someone or you've got children, that you can work the hours to suit round what you've got to do outside. Our company encourages that." (Male shop steward, 60 yrs, fitter)

Among those who offered some kind of explanation for flexible working there was great variation in their accounts. Seven shop stewards simply offered explanations in relation to 'flexitime' – flexible start and finish times – but they did not show familiarity with other aspects of flexible working or with reasons for using it.

The remaining 10 stewards were unable to offer any kind of explanation for the term and responded to the interviewer with blank expressions or shrugs. This seems surprising as, at the time of interviewing, the AEEU had begun to include flexible working in their training programmes for shop stewards.

Around half of those who had some understanding of flexible working also held quite negative views towards it. These shop stewards felt that there was a link between flexible working and being multiskilled, thus being flexible in the workplace. This involves employees being trained in various skills in order that the workforce is more flexible. Most workers felt negatively towards this; it appeared to threaten their identity as having a particular type of job. To illustrate:

"Flexible working, I suppose, is being able to do my job and go and do someone else's job. They're trying to make manufacturing leaner, everyone being able to do everyone else's job." (Male shop steward, 38 yrs, machine setter)

Those who felt negatively also expressed views that flexible working had to be a two-way process between employee and employer for it to work. However, their experience of it was that it only benefited the employer, who could have employees working flat out at prime time and fewer hours when orders are low to keep costs down. This meant a very inflexible and insecure working pattern for the employee:

"It's giving you flexibility in your time off but it's not giving it. Their argument with flexible working was that everyone would turn in the morning and they'd turn round and say, 'Right we don't need you, you, or you, you go home and come back tonight' ... That's their flexible working." (Male shop steward, 37 yrs, engineering technician)

"My understanding of flexible working is that if you're working in the manufacturing industry when orders are good, then obviously they want all hands to the pump. However, the employer wants flexibility when things are not so good to give him the scope to keep costs down for the employer, to be competitive in the market-place. It affects people's income because most of the time people work 40 hours a

week. With flexibility, they can work 20 if the work does drop off, and then the wages reduce by half. At the end of the day, they've still got a family to maintain, they've still got overheads; their bills don't decrease – it's very difficult." (Male shop steward, 31 yrs, process operator)

Family-friendly or flexible working?

Once the shop stewards had given their views on flexible working, they were read the definition of flexible working practices used in the questionnaire study (see Chapter 2). They were then asked whether they personally preferred the term 'family-friendly working' or 'flexible working' and why. Figure 3.1 shows the distribution of their responses. Eleven shop stewards said that they preferred 'family-friendly' and the key reason for this was that they felt that this seemed to indicate an employee benefit rather than a company benefit.

"Family-friendly working is when it's discussed openly and agreed. Flexibility is more thrust on you than negotiated with." (Male shop steward, 43 yrs, motor vehicle fitter)

"Family-friendly, I would regard as actually fitting in with family needs, whereas flexible working may fit in with commercial needs." (Male shop steward, 46 yrs, electrician, joiner)

Figure 3.1: Preferred terms

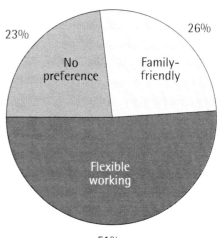

23% No preference
26% Family-friendly
51% Flexible working

"It comes down on the side of trying to benefit your children, whereas the other one seems to be more to benefit the company." (Male shop steward, 39 yrs, maintenance fitter)

Just over half the shop stewards (22) preferred the term 'flexible working', mainly because it indicated that flexible benefits were for the whole workforce, not just those with families:

"Not everyone's got a family ... some people are quite alone but would still prefer to do flexi-working time." (Female shop steward, 57 yrs, panel wirer)

Within this group, there were also views that making the term more general would make it more acceptable or, in the case of the following shop steward, 'honest'.

"Flexible working is more honest ... not just for the family, maybe for their sporting pleasure, for themselves ... let's be honest then we can trust each other." (Male shop steward, 42 yrs, production manager)

"Family-friendly working would penalise people who are not part of a family and they have just as much right to flexibility for social functions, sport, education etc." (Male shop steward, 54 yrs, maintenance fitter)

In addition, 'flexible' was felt to be more gender-neutral than 'family'.

"If you start talking about family-friendly working then you'd start raising gender and equality issues because then I think people will think, oh they're women and therefore they have got to have this family-friendly thing." (Female shop steward, 44 yrs, service operations assistant)

Ten shop stewards did not feel either term was appropriate and this view was mostly held among those who had already expressed a negative view towards the principle of flexible working.

"If you feel your home life is more important than your job, perhaps you shouldn't be doing that job." (Male shop steward, 48 yrs, senior estate officer)

"Family-friendly working is terminology that would be used by managers in order to con the workforce. Flexible working encompasses doing other people's jobs. I don't like either term." (Male shop steward, 52 yrs, maintenance electrician)

Flexibility depends on your job

One recurring theme that emerged in the interviews was that the suitability and success of flexible working depended more on the type of job that was to be done than on the gender of the worker. Three quarters of the shop stewards interviewed felt that flexible working was workable for office staff, but not for those who work in manufacturing or engineering. It was acknowledged that such staff also tend to be female, but it was the nature of the work that appeared to be important. This view was also linked to a view that flexible working and shift work were incompatible.

"You'll find the clerical staff use it a lot more ... they may agree it with their local manager. It seems to work a lot better for them; it's easier for them to work round it." (Male shop steward, 48 yrs, mechanical engineer)

Shift work

The majority of shop stewards raised shift working as a significant barrier to the implementation of flexible working. A traditional male-dominated workforce within the engineering sector is accustomed to shift working patterns that are predictable and fixed. One shop steward made the point that he could tell us when he would be working this time next year and that these fixed (rather than flexible) shifts offered him predictability, which actually enabled him to spend time with his children, from whom he was geographically separated. Many shop stewards expressed a view that men liked shift work because it was predictable and allowed them to plan leisure activities in their time away from work. There was also a view that if shift working resulted in men not being able to be involved in caring and domestic work, then this was perceived as a positive outcome for many men.

"With shift work, you know where you are. I know what shifts I'm working next year, so for organising your time, planning holidays, then shifts work. I feel they are a better choice than flexible working." (Male shop steward, 37 yrs, engineering technician)

There was a clear view that flexible working was not at all suitable for shift workers on a factory production line. This view was explained in terms of work that involves production or cover for 24 hours, seven days a week. The commonly held view was that flexible working would result in gaps in the assembly line or the team because people had elected to use their right to flexible working. There was concern that a flexible working pattern would make working times difficult to control and would risk shifts being either over- or under-staffed. Teamwork would be detrimentally affected.

"In the manufacturing industry you cannot have different people working at different times. You need the shift to produce the product that they've got." (Male shop steward, 37 yrs, maintenance fitter)

"Flexitime has its place in offices but certainly not on a shift system. People would just be coming in and out all the time. You're working in an ongoing production environment and there's safety and disciplines to be adhered to, you know, so I don't think that would work at all." (Male shop steward, 31 yrs, process operator)

Most felt that if a flexible working pattern were to have any chance of working within a shift system, then more staff would have to be employed to keep the lines covered, and that this would both increase productivity costs and reduce the opportunity for overtime.

Some felt that shifts were bad for their general health, but what came across most strongly was that the popularity or otherwise of shift work depended on the type of shift pattern to which employees were subjected. Some did not like their shift pattern because they always felt too tired on their days off to do anything else but recover. Others did not like their shifts because they resulted in time off when friends and family were at work and the children at school. Others

felt that a shift system of working four days on and having four off gave them too much time off when they often found themselves having to help out at home! However, the majority did like their shifts because they gave them adequate time to pursue sport and hobbies. Also, many people mentioned that their shifts provided a structure that they liked. They knew where they were with their shifts, whereas they felt a system of flexible working would mean they would lose this predictability.

The relationship between fixed shifts and flexible working may reveal an important issue for the future of family-friendly arrangements. Those who have caring responsibilities require flexibility, often at short notice. Shift working may provide a form of flexibility in that it usually results in work outside the nine-to-five pattern but the working pattern of shift workers is often difficult to change. While some of the shop stewards interviewed expressed a view that fixed shifts were helpful for those with caring responsibilities as it allowed them to predict and organise care, others stated a clear view that certain types of employment involved working patterns that could not be flexible and were incompatible with caring responsibilities.

The interviews revealed an ethos of traditional employment practices, which are predictable and fixed, but with opportunities for overtime. There seemed to be a strong sense that more flexible employment was consistent with people simply turning up for work when they felt like it. This view was also linked to the belief that it was only acceptable for women to work within engineering and manufacturing if they did so within a structure of traditional employment practices.

Overtime

A key concern for many shop stewards was the effect that the implementation of a flexible working pattern would have on overtime. Many shift workers rely on their overtime to supplement their income, and were aware that a flexible working system could mean the end of overtime. From a business perspective, this might be an asset, but from the employees' point of view, losing the opportunity to do overtime was seen as very negative by 80% of shop stewards interviewed.

"People will work Saturdays to get the overtime, but they won't work Saturdays on a flexible working system without overtime." (Male shop steward, 43 yrs, meter fixer)

"If you're all working flexibly, you're not working as much overtime so you're giving up all your prime time. At the moment we work weekends and we get overtime. That's the biggest thing really." (Male shop steward, 31 yrs, process operator)

Concerns about loss of overtime and changes to shift work are understandable in the context of current UK working patterns. The male worker within a traditional male-dominated workforce, working long hours and using overtime as a means of providing essential family income, relies on the extra income. The need for more balance between work and life outside work was more likely to be highlighted by older shop stewards who no longer needed to support their children:

"The overtime payment is good, but it's not good for your home life. Someone younger, maybe they want more overtime. Me, I prefer the time off. The part of the company I work in is quite flexible; I work a flexible system that allows me to work 37 hours flexible start and finish time and flexible time off. If there's a need for a 24-hour production then you've got to have a 24-hour shift, but I work on maintenance." (Male shop steward, 51 yrs, bricklayer)

Summary

- One fifth of shop stewards interviewed did not know what flexible working was.
- The concept of flexible working is often viewed with suspicion, and as being predominantly in the employer's interest.
- Traditional male patterns of work such as shift work and overtime are seen to be under threat from flexible working.
- The majority of shop stewards preferred the term 'flexible' to 'family-friendly' when describing patterns of work designed to improve work–life balance.

Employment benefits and family life

The key aim of our research was to examine attitudes to flexible working, and to explore the relationship between work attitudes and the intention to use flexible working. Before examining general views about flexible working, we wanted to investigate the views of AEEU members about a wide variety of specific employment rights and benefits. We also wanted to investigate attitudes to work and family life by examining preferences for how families can divide work and childcare. In this and subsequent chapters, we compare the views held by men and women, those with and without caring responsibilities, and the views of those at different occupational levels.

Employment rights and benefits

Part of our questionnaire survey asked respondents to complete a table that listed specific employment rights and a wide variety of employment benefits.[3] Our aim was to provide as inclusive a list as possible and to list options that could be considered family-friendly (for example, workplace nursery) as well as those which might be unrelated to family needs (for example, retail vouchers). Respondents were asked to consider each item in a general way – 'taking all things into consideration' as to how good each would be from both an employer and employee perspective. They were asked to rate, on a 7-point scale, whether they thought the benefit was very poor (1) to very good (7).

A total of 1,669 respondents completed this part of the questionnaire, a slightly lower response than for other aspects of the questionnaire, possibly due to the large number of different options they were asked to consider.

Appendix A4.1, A4.2, A4.3 and A4.4, list the full range of items respondents were asked to consider, alongside the means and statistical differences between men and women, occupational levels, and carers and non-carers. Overall preferences and significant differences between groups will be discussed later.

Preferred employment rights and benefits

Figure 4.1 shows all the possible rights and benefits that respondents were asked to rate. The graph presents these in rank order with the most preferred option to the left. The most popular option was a contributory pension scheme, followed by paid time off for emergencies within the family, statutory maternity leave, the choice of whether to do overtime, and extra holiday entitlement – these five options all gained approval by over 80% of respondents. Least popular were unpaid paternity leave, school term-time only contracts, unpaid career breaks, retail vouchers, company car, and working at home – these six options gained approval from only 40-50% of respondents.

It is clear that all the options had reasonable approval ratings – the mean rating given to all the options was above the midpoint of 4, thus overall our respondents did not feel that the options were negative. However, it is interesting that – with the exception of statutory maternity

---

[3] Our questionnaire survey was conducted prior to the changes in statutory rights for parents which came into effect in April 2003. Appendix B shows the pre-2003 and current employment rights for people with children.

leave – the top five options were generic benefits that, if available, would be aimed at the entire workforce, not just at mothers or those with small children. Parental leave was rated positively by only 71.3% of respondents whereas the more general 'time off for emergencies within the family' was rated positively by 83.1%.

This initial analysis, from this predominantly male workforce, would appear to indicate that general work–life balance policies aimed at the whole workforce might gain greater acceptance than those targeted at specific groups.

Differences between men and women

There were a number of differences between men and women in their ratings of a number of employment rights and benefits. These are documented in Appendix A4.3. Figure 4.2 shows those that had the highest levels of statistically

Figure 4.1: Judgements on rights and benefits

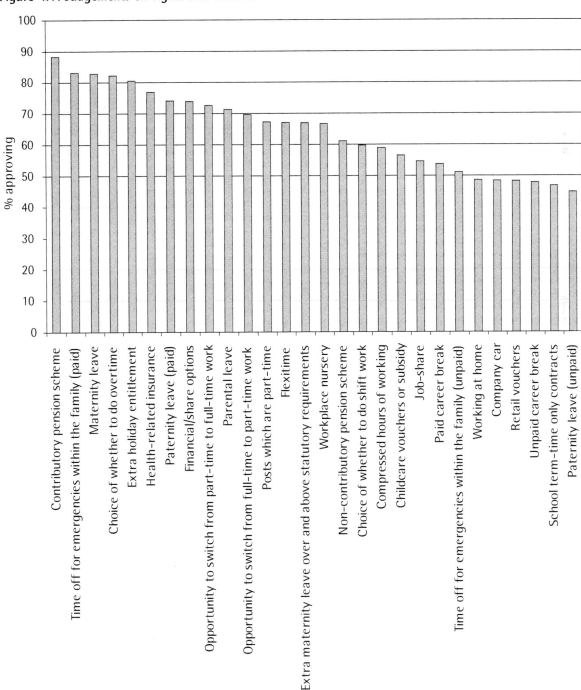

Benefit type

significant differences (*p*<0.001). Men showed a greater preference than women for paid time off for emergencies within the family. In the case of all other highly significant differences women showed greater approval levels than men. Mostly these differences related to flexibility in working hours – job-share, term-time only working, part-time working and the ability to move between full- and part-time work. These findings are interesting in the context of this being a sample of full-time workers. It seems that even those women who work full-time feel more positively than men about flexible working hours and part-time working. Women also showed a greater preference than men for statutory maternity leave and workplace nursery provision.

Figure 4.2: Differences in men's and women's approval of employment rights and benefits opportunities

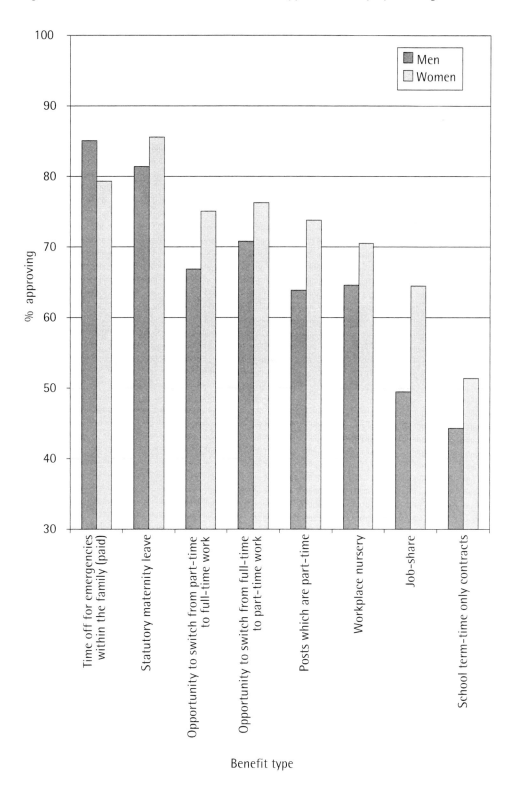

Differences as a function of occupational level

For almost every employment right or benefit, there were significant differences between the groups, with approval ratings for particular benefits generally increasing with occupational level. Figure 4.3 shows those which have the most highly significant differences between these groups. Some of the greatest differences arose in approval of working practices that allowed greater flexibility in hours or place of work – part-time working, flexitime and working at home. The differences in unpaid paternity leave were echoed in the ratings of paid paternity leave – approval for this declines with occupational level, but declines most sharply in the case of unpaid leave. Appendix A4.3 gives a detailed breakdown of all the differences in approval levels between managerial, skilled and semi-skilled workers.

The differences in the approval of paid career breaks are most likely related to the improbability of these being offered to non-managerial employees. A similar explanation may be likely for the differences in approval of

non-contributory pension schemes, as these are more likely to be available to employees in managerial and skilled occupations. However, as the questionnaire instructions asked respondents to consider each option at a general rather than at a personal level, it seems surprising that the benefits of such schemes were not appreciated by over 50% of semi-skilled workers.

Carers and non-carers

Differences in the views of those who had caring responsibilities for a child, elderly person or disabled person and those had no caring responsibilities were also examined. Differences between carers and non-carers were much fewer than between men and women and between occupational levels. Figure 4.4 shows all the statistically significant differences. Not surprisingly these are almost entirely related to leave for parental responsibilities or working hours that fit with school term-times.

Figure 4.3: Differences in approval of employment rights and benefits as a function of occupational level

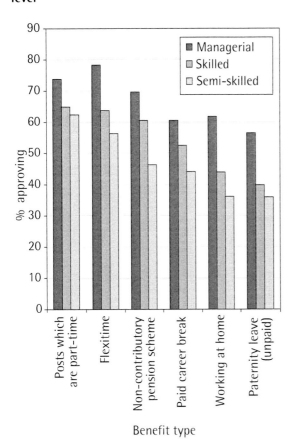

Figure 4.4: Differences between non-carers' and carers' approval of employment rights and benefits

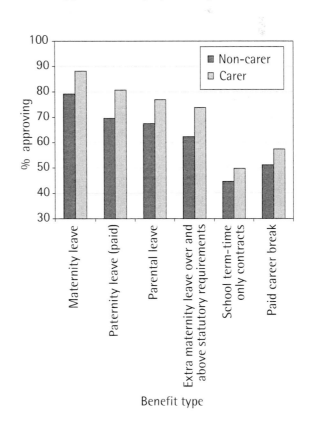

Preferences for work and family life

We were interested in examining attitudes to how work and family life might be divided between men and women. Our questionnaire survey asked respondents to consider six different options under the following instructions: In Britain today, families combine work and family life in different ways. If all these resulted in the same amount of income, how much would each suit you?

Respondents rated each option in terms of how much they felt each would suit them personally on a scale of not at all (1) to very much (7).

Overall, the most strongly preferred option for work and family life was for both parents to work flexibly and to share childcare and domestic work. This was followed by the most prevalent situation in the UK at present: father works full-time and mother works part-time. However, women were more likely than men to prefer sharing both work and childcare using flexible working. Figure 4.5 shows the preferences of men and women for each option. Appendix A4.5 and A4.6 shows a detailed breakdown of preferences by gender, occupational level and caring responsibilities.

The most striking aspect of these findings is that even among respondents from traditional and male-dominated occupations, there is a growing recognition that family life might be improved if men and women were able to share work and family responsibilities more evenly.

Figure 4.5: Judgements about types of family–work arrangements

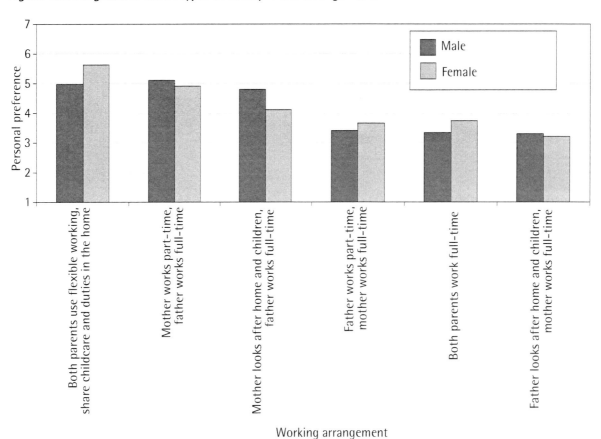

Summary

- A contributory pension scheme, paid time off for emergencies in the family, and statutory maternity leave were the three most popular employment rights and benefits.
- In general there were stronger preferences for general employment benefits – pensions, extra holiday entitlement and health insurance – than for policies that provided flexibility in working hours or locations.
- Women had significantly higher approval ratings than men for flexibility in working hours – job-share, term-time only working, part-time working and the ability to move between full- and part-time work.
- Those with any kind of caring responsibility were more strongly in favour of rights and benefits for working parents.
- Approval of all employment rights and benefits increased with occupational level; managers felt most positive about all the options available, with the exception of retail vouchers.
- Women's most strongly preferred option for work and family life was for both parents to work flexibly and to share childcare and work in the home. Men were also strongly in favour of this option.

5

Attitudes and intentions towards flexible working arrangements

This chapter describes the caring responsibilities of those who responded to our questionnaire survey and then examines respondents' beliefs about flexible working. We compare the views held by men and women, those with and without caring responsibilities, and those at different occupational levels. Current use of flexible working and intention to use flexible working in the future are also examined. Finally we examine how attitudes and demographic factors relate to intention to use flexible working in the future and illustrate our findings in a model.

Men and women

In the UK in 2001, 91% of employed men worked full-time compared to only 56% of women (ONS, 2001). There has been little change in the proportion of women working part-time in the 1990s despite higher employment rates among women with young children. Working part-time has been the most widely available form of flexible working over a number of decades. Men tend to work part-time at the beginning or end of their employment history, whereas the proportion of women working part-time varies less across different age groups. Despite decades of part-time working by women, men have shown a consistently low uptake of part-time work; this may mean that men may be less likely to use other forms of flexible working in the future. The present study was able to examine the extent to which men and women who are currently in full-time work use, and intend to use, flexible working options.

While the prevalence of part-time working for women varies in different countries (Eurostat, 2000), research into gender differences has

continued to conclude that men are socialised to give priority to the breadwinner role, whereas women are socialised to give priority to homemaker and motherhood roles (Lewis, 1992; Major, 1993). Hakim (2000) has argued that the majority of women (around 60%) are 'adaptive' – they want to work but are not totally committed to a career, and are thus more likely to work part-time and to make use of flexible working policies.

The attitudes that women hold towards work and the family may partly explain reasons as to why women may be more likely than men to use flexible working. In a small-scale qualitative study, Warin et al (1999) examined attitudes to work and family life and found that women often gave very different reasons to men for participating in paid work:

> Women did not often stress the issue of money and were more likely to mention the social side of work, getting out of the house, enjoyment, a sense of achievement and independence. Men did mention some of these rewards, but were very much more likely to talk about their work in terms of the financial rewards it offered and to relate it to their providing role in the family.
> (Warin et al, 1999, p 14)

Warin et al (1999) found a strong emphasis on the provider role for fathers in families and they suggest that one particular policy implication of these findings is that there should be more promotion of men's roles as parents, rather than simply as providers. Thus attitudes to, and uptake of, flexible working policies may reflect attitudes to parenthood as well as work.

Despite, or perhaps because of, the findings that women appear to place greater emphasis on domesticity than on a professional working role, Goodstein (1994) found that working women are one of the most important groups influencing companies to adopt flexible working programmes. The need for flexible working arrangements is often perceived as a women's issue, and much of what has been written about them has been in response to the question of how to make organisations more family-friendly for women (see Cook, 1992). Many male employees are hesitant to voice family-related concerns for fear that these concerns will conflict with the corporate image of a successful male (Powell, 1997). From this, one might conclude that managers may be more likely to grant family-friendly working arrangements to female than male subordinates because they believe that such arrangements are more appropriate for women than men. Indeed, Reynolds et al (2003) reported that some male employees do feel that this occurs. Powell and Mainiero (1999) conducted a study in which participants were asked to assume themselves in the role of manager when reading vignettes that described a subordinate making a request for an alternative working arrangement. Fifty-three current or past managers participated when they enrolled in an evening MBA programme. Powell and Mainiero found that managers were equally likely to grant requests by either gender; however, female managers were more likely to support alternative working arrangements in a way that their male counterparts did not. Given this, it would appear that women have a greater concern with striking a balance between work and family than men (Powell and Mainiero, 1999). Further, because female managers may themselves need flexible working arrangements at some point in their careers, they may be more inclined towards them than male managers.

The typical pattern of family employment in the UK is therefore one of fathers who work long hours and mothers who work in low-paid, part-time jobs (Dex, 1999). Unless men begin to accept and use the family-friendly benefits, it is likely that current gender divisions in work will amplify. This would further create a gender-differentiated workforce of women who need flexibility and make use of family-friendly policies and men who provide employers with flexibility and avoid using policies that they fear

may undermine their opportunities for advancement and promotion.

Those with caring responsibilities

One aim of flexible working arrangements is to enable those with caring responsibilities to engage in paid work. While raising children is one source of caring responsibility, the baseline study of work–life balance practices in Britain (Hogarth et al, 2000) showed that 15% of women employees and 11% of male employees have caring responsibilities for someone other than their children. It seems likely that those with caring responsibilities may feel more positively towards flexible working than those who have no such responsibilities. However, the use of flexible working practices may raise issues of fairness for those who do not have caring responsibilities.

According to US employee surveys, programmes that provide all employees with alternatives to the traditional full-time, fixed hour and fixed place work arrangements are clearly preferred over other types of work–family programmes that are aimed specifically at dependent care (Friedman and Galinsky, 1992).

Occupational level

Occupational level tends to define the structure of working patterns. This is perhaps more marked within the electrical and engineering sector than in others. Managerial staff often have no set hours of work and do not have to keep a record of their hours. However, they are usually required to work outside normal working hours if a task requires it. Managerial staff have to ensure that work is conducted to an adequate standard and often have to ensure that performance targets are met. Work at a managerial level tends to be subject to evaluation in terms of the quality of work – how well it is done. Skilled workers can have very variable working patterns; some will be required to clock in and out of factories. In this case, work will take place within the confines of specific hours and locations, everyone will go home when the factory closes and it is not possible to 'take work home'. Other skilled workers may find their days defined by specific tasks rather than prescribed hours. There may be a job sheet with a number of electric fires to install, gas boilers to fit or cars to repair. In these cases the skilled worker will experience more autonomy, but also more pressure to ensure that the jobs are completed. Thus it may be possible to take a longer lunch break after a relatively straightforward job or to move onto the next job in anticipation of finishing early. However, there is also some requirement to complete work within a time period, thus necessitating some flexibility in start and finish times according to the jobs being done. Semi and unskilled workers are most likely to have to work to rigid working hours, which are monitored, and to have pay allocated per hour worked. In this context there may be little scope for producing work of variable quality, with performance being more likely to be evaluated in terms of reliability and consistency.

Given the varied nature of work for different occupational levels, it seems likely that managers, skilled workers and semi-skilled workers will have different experiences of, and attitudes towards, flexible working.

Examining attitudes in the questionnaire survey

It was clear from our interviews with shop stewards that it was possible for employees to experience quite conflicting views about flexible working. They might feel quite positive about the impact of flexible working on their own lives, but recognise that this would not necessarily be positive for colleagues or their employer. Similarly employees may feel that flexible working would enable them to spend more time with their family, but also that it would prevent them being promoted at work. Our survey included questions designed to measure different aspects of people's views about flexible working, rather than simply how positively people felt towards such policies in general.

Respondents were also asked the extent to which they felt their current working arrangements were flexible and how much they felt that they would like to use flexible working in the future. We compared the views of men and women, those with and without caring responsibilities, and different occupational groups – managerial

workers, skilled workers and semi-skilled workers.

All differences reported in this chapter are statistically significant at least at the 0.001 level of significance unless otherwise stated. Therefore the results are generally highly reliable statistically.

Caring: a heavy burden borne by few?

Respondents were asked to indicate how many hours each week they spent caring for children and sick/elderly/disabled people. We analysed the data to see whether the subgroup of people with children differed from the larger group of carers and found no substantive differences. We then considered whether carers and non-carers would differ in their attitudes and intentions towards flexible working. For the purposes of this study, anyone who indicated any level of caring responsibility for a child, disabled person, elderly person or other person was classified as a 'carer'.

Caring responsibilities

A higher proportion of men (44%) than women (32%) reported having some caring responsibilities, a highly significant difference that was even larger when focusing purely on childcare (33% as against 17%). This may seem surprising, but must be interpreted in the context of this being a survey of full-time workers. Caring responsibilities, particularly for children, are likely to result in women working part-time; those in full-time work are less likely to be those with caring responsibilities. Despite fewer women reporting caring responsibilities than men, we found a dramatic schism in the pattern of caring responsibilities. Among people with caring responsibilities, women devoted an average of 39.2 hours per week to caring, whereas men devoted an average of 17.4 hours per week. This highly significant difference remained constant within all three levels of employee classification, and when age was accounted for (see Appendix A5.1).

In summary, in this sample of full-time workers, women were between half and three quarters as likely as men to report having caring responsibilities, but women who did have such responsibilities devoted twice as much time to them as men did. Indeed, women with caring responsibilities devoted the equivalent of a full-time working week to caring. These patterns in the sample show that men are much less differentiated than women within the workforce in terms of whether they have caring commitments.

Flexible working

Current use of flexible working practices

On a scale from 1 (not at all) to 7 (very much), carers reported being marginally more likely (mean = 2.70) than non-carers (mean = 2.51) to make use of flexible working. However, the more substantial differences were attributable to gender (males mean = 2.70, females mean = 2.37) and occupational level (managerial mean = 3.03, skilled mean = 2.45, semi-skilled mean = 2.19).

When considered as a percentage of people who scored above the scale midpoint (that is, did use flexible working regularly), the occupational differences are clear: 29% of managerial, 19% of skilled and 15% of semi-skilled workers used flexible working. Moreover, the gender difference was statistically reliable only among semi-skilled workers. Twenty per cent of semi-skilled men but only 10% of semi-skilled women used flexible working. Therefore, the primary determinant of uptake of flexible working opportunities was occupational level rather than gender or caring responsibilities. In this sample of full-time workers, those least likely to use flexible working were semi-skilled women.

Intention to use flexible working practices

Intentions to use flexible working were measured on a scale from 1 to 7 (strongly disagree to strongly agree). Overall, there was a high level of intention to use flexible working (mean = 5.47), with 72% saying they would intend to use flexible working, given the option.

Caring responsibilities were not associated with intentions to use flexible working. However, there were statistically significant differences in the responses made by men and women, and more substantial differences associated with

different occupational levels. Women were slightly more likely to intend to use flexible working. Managerial workers were more likely to intend to use flexible working (80%) than either skilled (70%) or semi-skilled (63%) workers (see Appendix A5.2).

Taken together, the measures of flexible working show that among this sample of full-time workers there was a strong desire generally to use flexible working. However, people higher up the occupational ladder are more likely both to use and to intend to use flexible working than those lower down.[4]

Attitudes to flexible working

We measured five aspects of attitudes to flexible working. These were whether it resulted in:

- *personal benefits* to employees (for example, to meet family responsibilities);
- *employer benefits* (for example, increased productivity);
- *employee success* (for example, promotion, respect for employees);
- *engagement* with the organisation (for example, lower absenteeism);
- *poor performance* (for example, employees lacking motivation).

We also examined two aspects of attitudes to *long working hours*:

- *positive* (for example, being considered as a good colleague);
- *negative* (for example, strain on family life).

The effects of gender, occupational level and whether or not the respondent was a carer on these seven types of measure were analysed using multivariate analysis of variance (MANOVA).

---

[4] Both actual use of flexible working and intention to use it if it were to become available were included as outcomes in the model presented on page 27. This is because actual use of flexible working may be strongly related to its availability, whereas intention to use it allows those who do not currently have this option to indicate a desire to do so.

Overall, participants expressed very positive attitudes and few reservations about flexible working practices. They felt personal benefits would be high (88% agree, mean = 5.81), that employers would benefit (72% agree, mean = 5.31), and that engagement would be improved (53% agree, mean = 4.54). They did not feel flexible working would result in poorer work performance (18% agree, mean = 3.00). They felt there were few benefits in long hours working (35% agree, mean = 3.65) and substantial negative consequences of long hours working (86% agree, mean = 5.60).

Despite these favourable attitudes, workers who agreed that flexible working would lead to employee success (21%) were outnumbered by more than two to one by those who disagreed (47%, mean = 3.61) (see Appendix A5.3 and A5.4).

Concerns that flexible working is incompatible with career success were also clear in the interview studies with shop stewards:

"Line managers lead people to believe that if they want to get on they won't claim flexitime...." (Female shop steward, 44 yrs, service operations assistant, no caring responsibilities)

"It's not just about success; it's about keeping your job. There's so much severance that I've done an 85-hour week to get the work done. I need my job." (Male shop steward, 42 yrs, production manager, no caring responsibilities)

Carers and non-carers differed significantly in their views of engagement (means = 4.68 and 4.45, respectively), employer benefits (means = 5.35 and 5.28, respectively) and negative aspects of long hours working (means = 5.70 and 5.53, respectively). Compared with non-carers, carers believed flexible working practices would do more to improve employees' engagement with the organisation, would benefit the employer more, and that there were more negative aspects of working long hours.

A substantial and highly significant gender difference emerged on personal benefits of flexible working (males mean = 5.69, females mean = 6.03), employer benefits (means = 5.14

Figure 5.1: Percentage of men and women who agree with beliefs about flexible working

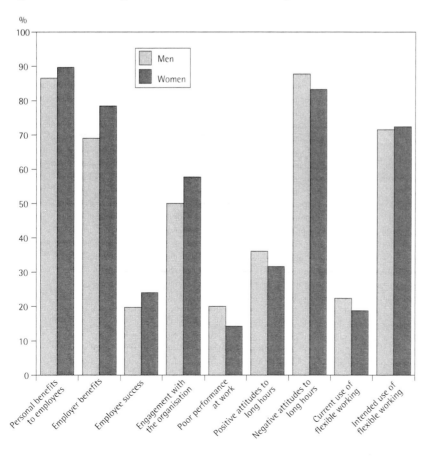

and 5.64, respectively), engagement (means = 4.43 and 4.74, respectively) and poorer work performance (means = 3.16 and 2.71, respectively). In sum, women held more positive views of flexible working than men did (see Figure 5.1).

The difference between carers and non-carers' attitudes towards work engagement also varied as a function of gender. The difference in men's and women's attitudes was much smaller among those without any caring responsibilities (male mean = 4.37, female mean = 4.56) than those with caring responsibilities (means = 4.51 and 5.15, respectively).

A significant difference between occupational groups emerged on personal benefits of flexible working. Managers felt these benefits would be greater (mean = 5.95) than did skilled (mean = 5.75) and semi-skilled workers (mean = 5.70), respectively. Managers also felt there would be less poor performance as a result of flexible work practices being available (means = 2.95, 3.05 and 2.99, respectively).

The significantly greater approval of flexible working among women is notable. Our interview study with shop stewards (Chapter 3) revealed the views of men who felt very negatively about flexible working and about women in the workforce. This was a sizeable group – around a quarter of those we interviewed. Our questionnaire survey shows that strongly negative views among men were not as prevalent as the interviews would have led one to expect, or may be associated with being a shop steward. Shop stewards' views are illustrated in the following quotations:

"I'm from a background where the man's the breadwinner. It's not the man who has the baby, and it's not the man who stays at home to care for the baby. So flexibility is aimed more at women than men. If a woman's had a baby, the man needs to work full-time anyway to support his family.... It's good for women who might be starting a family, to go part-time or job-share. That would make home life a lot easier. But if we go too far down the job-share line, there won't be any full-time jobs left!" (Male shop steward, 26 yrs, foundry operative)

"It infuriates me when I have to listen to women who are continually asking for equal opportunities in everything and yet expect preferential treatment. I have no trouble with one or the other but I don't like double standards. This is how flexible working and work–life balance comes across in the media." (Male shop steward, 45 yrs, mechanic/technician)

"I think flexible working is a con-trick, perpetuated by employers. It's an excuse by women to undermine shift working and shift pay, reducing payments. Traditionally, I would be on double time working Sundays, and people are nowhere near approaching that now. It started with women working in shops, now men are on the checkouts more and more. Flexible working is undermining my position and that of my members in long, hard-argued agreements." (Male shop steward, 52 yrs, maintenance electrician)

Effects of gender, caring responsibilities, occupational level and attitudes on current and intended flexible working

What predicts people's intentions to use flexible working?

In order to predict people's intentions to use flexible working we used a multiple regression approach. First, we assessed the combined effects of gender, caring and occupational level on the attitudes described above. Second, we examined whether all of these variables would predict how much the respondents currently use, and intend to use, flexible working practices (see Appendix A5.5).

This analysis tells us that the combined effect of gender, occupational level and caring did not account for more than 4% of the variation in any of the attitudes toward flexible working. Second, the stronger relationships are between gender and attitudes. Third, employees' expectations that flexible working increases employee success are not related to occupational level. Therefore one conclusion is that these attitudes to flexible working practices are likely to be developed through experiences that are not distinctive to particular genders, particular occupational levels or particular caring responsibilities. Instead, other factors seem likely to underpin attitudes to flexible working.

The next set of analyses used hierarchical multiple regression procedures (Appendix A5.6) to explore how age, gender, occupational level, caring and attitudes were associated with existing use of flexible working and intended use of flexible working. In the first step we tested the effects of gender, occupational level and caring. Managerial occupational level predicted current use of flexible working. Age, gender, managerial occupational level and caring were all independently associated with employees' intended use of flexible working. However, in both analyses the total amount of variance accounted for was just 3%.

In the second step we added the attitude measures to predict actual and intended use of flexible working. In the case of intended working we also included whether they were already using flexible working as a predictor.

Once these attitude measures were included, the effects of occupational level and gender were both reduced slightly, indicating that some part of those effects is mediated by attitudes. More importantly, attitudes independently accounted for a more substantial part of the variation in employees' current and intended use of flexible working. This can be seen from the change from step 1 to step 2 in the cumulative R^2 statistics. After age, gender, occupational level and caring were controlled, attitudes explained a further 4% of the variance in current working, and 24% of the variance in employees' intentions (see Appendix A5.6).

In summary, current use of flexible working was associated most strongly with managerial occupations, the belief that flexible working would benefit employers and the perception that flexible working would lead to success.

Intentions to use flexible working in future were associated to some extent with managerial occupations and with current use of flexible working. However, the stronger relationships were between intentions and the perception that flexible working would bring personal benefits, would increase engagement with the

organisation, and with rejection of the idea that it would result in poorer work performance. Remarkably, these attitudes accounted for nearly 10 times the amount of variation in employees' intention to work flexibly than was explained by age, gender, occupational level and caring responsibilities alone.

On the basis of these findings we suggest a causal model of these relationships (Figure 5.2).[5] The presence of significant statistical associations is depicted by the solid lines with arrows. Figure 5.2 also shows, with broken lines, other factors that could influence current and intended use of flexible working. Because the effects of the demographic variables are rather weak, it seems likely that there must be other variables that affect both employee attitudes and their intentions to use flexible working. For example, it seems likely that characteristics of the person, such as their personality, motivation, or particular relationships that they have with others, could influence their attitudes to flexible working. Similarly it seems likely that features that are specific to a person's occupation or organisation, and their role within it, may influence their attitudes. It is also possible that personal and workplace factors affect people's intentions directly. For example, a person's skills and qualifications, or other commitments, may determine their intentions regardless of their attitudes. Likewise, organisational policy or regulations may enforce, or prevent, uptake of flexible working practices regardless of a person's attitudes. We will consider some of these possibilities in a later chapter. For the time being, however, it seems reasonable to conclude that there is a substantial and important social psychological component underlying people's intentions to pursue flexible working, and that these may exist somewhat independently of a person's gender, occupational level or caring responsibilities.

---

[5] Our analysis is based on cross-sectional data and strictly speaking cannot support a causal model. We outline a model which is consistent with our findings. Our interpretation of the possible causal connections are consistent with the evidence from our interviews.

Figure 5.2: Model depicting the effect of demographic and attitudinal variables on current and intended use of flexible working practices

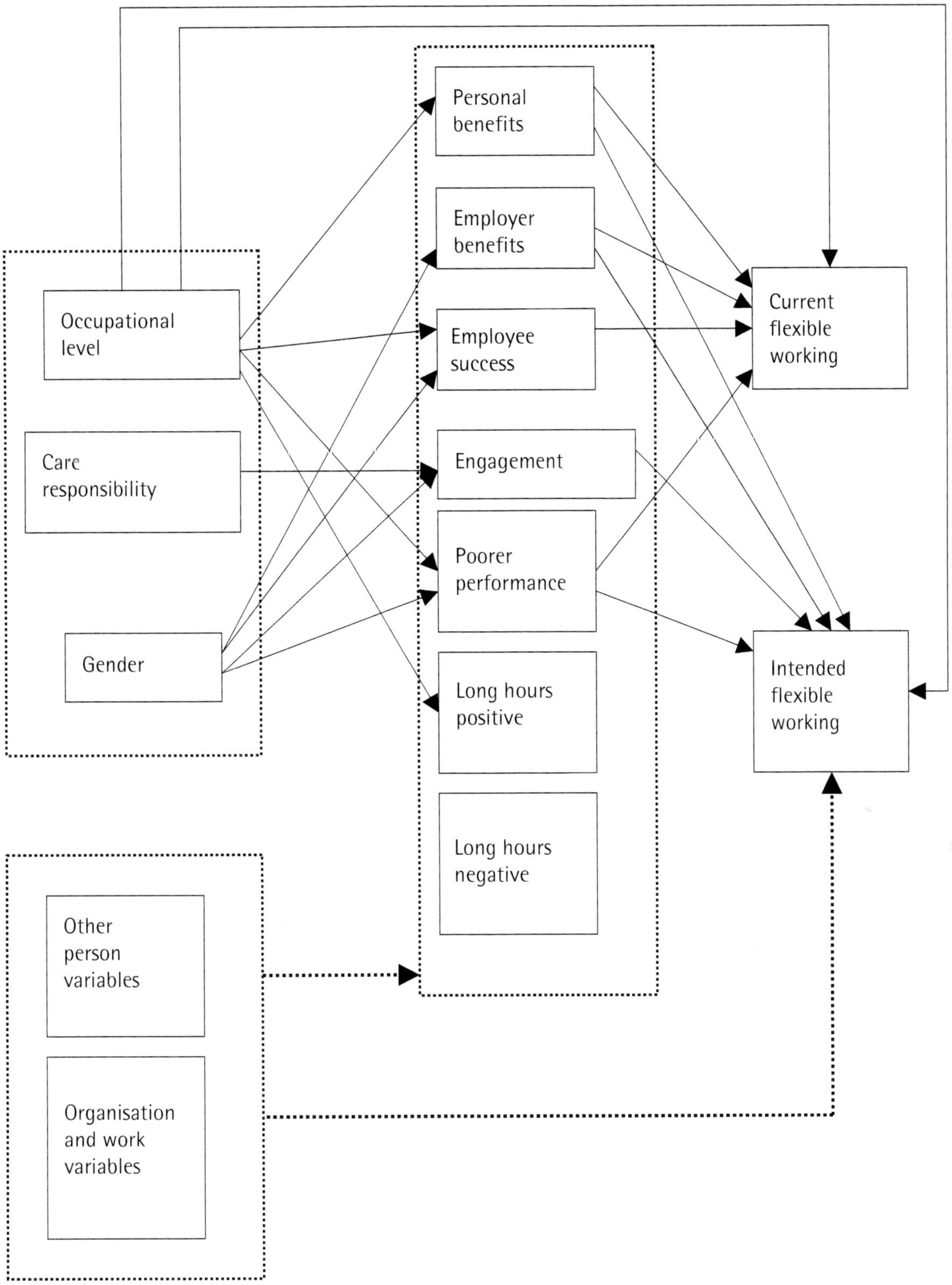

Note: Solid lines depict known statistical associations. Dotted boxes contain conceptually related variables. Dotted lines depict possible effects of other non-specified variables.

Summary

- Fewer women than men in this sample of full-time workers claim to have caring responsibilities.
- Women who care for dependants devote a very substantial amount of time to caring, more than double that of men with caring responsibilities. This is despite the fact that all the respondents in the sample were working full-time.
- Carers and non-carers made similar use of flexible working practices.
- Male managers were most likely, and female semi-skilled workers least likely, to be current users of flexible working practices.
- The majority of employees (72%) intended to use flexible working in the future if possible – women more so than men, and managers more so than skilled or semi-skilled workers.
- Women feel more positively about flexible working than men.
- Employees expressed strong expectations that flexible working would be good for the employer and employee, particularly among female and managerial employees. However, the majority also disagreed that flexible working would lead to respect and promotion.
- Attitudes were strongly associated with intentions to use flexible working. Employees who perceived greater personal benefits, better engagement with the organisation and fewer negative work outcomes expressed the strongest intentions to use flexible working practices.
- Other personal and organisational factors are likely to affect attitudes and intentions to pursue flexible working practices. These will be explored in subsequent chapters.

Family, stress and conflict

6

In this chapter we examine our survey respondents' experiences of conflict and support in work and family life, stress and ill-health. We examine differences between men and women, carers and non-carers, and those at different occupational levels. We then examine the relationship between these personal characteristics, flexible working and another possible outcome – intentions to leave their organisation.

Conflict between work and family life

The difficulties in balancing work and family life have been the subject of a growing amount of research since the 1990s. While most workers report that family is more important than work, research indicates that the experience of work conflicting with family is greater than family conflicting with work (Gutek et al, 1988, 1991; Judge et al, 1994). Extended working hours have also been linked to work–family conflict (Piotrkowski et al, 1987).

Research literature has portrayed work–family balance as a sense of having been able to meet the multiple demands of work and family responsibilities (Kahn et al, 1964; Greenhaus and Beutell, 1985). However, role expectations are not always compatible. Theorists such as Karasek (1979) have proposed that men fulfil their family roles by being good providers and spending more time at work; therefore, work expectations do not conflict with their family role expectations. The same model proposes that women experience greater conflict when they work because the family expectations that society places on them conflict with expectations placed on them at work. Although many women are employed, societal expectations for them to

remain domestically efficient and to spend more time at home persist nonetheless. For economic and social reasons, women are increasing their involvement in the workplace, thereby limiting the time they have available to perform their family roles. At the same time, men are beginning to share responsibilities for childcare and household chores in ways, it has been argued, that are causing them to re-evaluate their priorities away from work (Pleck, 1985). Eagle et al (1998) found that women did not experience disproportionately greater levels of work-to-family conflict or family-to-work conflict than men. Men reported greater work-to-family conflict than the women. Findings supported the interpretation offered by Duxbury et al (1991) that men may be finding it more difficult to balance increasing family demands because of greater work expectations made by their employers.

Frone et al (1992) reported work-to-family conflict to be directly related to alcohol problems while, more specifically, Frone et al (1994) demonstrated a link between lack of family time and compulsive drinking and smoking in employed mothers. Some evidence also suggests that parents' lack of time serves to diminish children's well-being (Belsky, 1990; Parcel and Menaghan, 1994). Results from studies examining the effects of parental work stress on children indicate that mothers tend to be emotionally and behaviourally withdrawn from their children on days when they reported a heavier workload, or where interpersonal conflict had occurred at work (Repetti and Wood, 1997). In an earlier study, Repetti (1994) examined the quality of fathers' interactions with older children and obtained similar results. Fathers' work experiences have also been demonstrated as having a more indirect influence on their children's behaviour, not only through parenting behaviour but also via job-related satisfaction, mood and tension (Stewart and Barling, 1996).

The ways in which family life may conflict with work, and work with family life, were measured using a questionnaire devised by Netemeyer et al (1996). As working long hours can lead to increased conflict we also examine hours of work in this chapter.

Family–work support

The research literature has focused on conflict between work and family; to date it has not explored the impact of family–work support. While conflict is an important area of inquiry, such an emphasis may serve to reinforce traditional views that family is incompatible with work. We hypothesised that many working people find that their family provides them with support in their working role. This may take the form of distraction or emotional closeness (for example, bathing the children at the end of the working day) or more explicit practical and emotional support for their working role (for example, discussing a work problem with a partner, or a child downloading and printing directions for the parent's business trip the following day). We therefore designed and piloted a short scale to measure the support that family can give to employees' work. We then investigated the role of support on work and personal outcomes.

Stress and ill-health

Stress is an adverse reaction to too much pressure. While pressure may occur in many aspects of life, the relationship between work and stress and the identification of specific work-related stressors are long established (Cox, 1978). Conflict, arising from the lack of workplace support for flexibility, including lack of childcare assistance, can be manifested in the mental health of employees. Lack of workplace flexibility has also been linked to depression in both women and men (Googins, 1991) and to increased physical distress, such as disturbed sleep, changes in appetite and muscular pain (Guelzow et al, 1991).

We examined experience of stress by measuring psychological health with a questionnaire and by examining days taken off work due to ill-health. The latter is a proxy measure of the physical and/ or mental health of an employee. Physical sickness may be unrelated to work factors, but can increase with stress or overwork (Cox, 1978). However, it is worth noting that is also possible that job-related factors or simply lack of work commitment can result in employees taking sickness absence when they are not unwell (Dex and Smith, 2002).

Turnover intention

Job satisfaction is known to be related to turnover intention – the intention to leave one's employer in the future (Hellman, 1997). Flexibility of employment and conflicts between work and family are also likely to influence intention to leave a job. Steel and Ovalle (1984) reported a strong relationship between turnover intention and turnover behaviour. Thus the intention to leave is a meaningful indicator of the employee's sense of commitment and satisfaction with their current employment.

Measures and overall pattern of responses

Work–family conflict was measured on a scale for which the mean scores can range from 1 to 7. It measures experiences where demands of work interfere with family life. The average score was 3.96, and 50% of the sample had scores above 4.

Family–work conflict was measured on a scale for which the mean scores can range from 1 to 7. Scores above 4 represent experiences where home or family life interferes with their work-related duties or responsibilities. The average score was 2.49; 10% of the sample had scores above the midpoint of 4.

Family–work support was measured using a scale for which the mean scores can range from 1 to 7. Scores above 4 mean that the person feels that their family provides them with support that helps their working role. The average score was 4.46, and 62% scored above 4.

Respondents were asked to report the average number of hours they spent at work each week.

Stress was measured using a scale for which the mean scores range from 0 to 3. Scores above 1 can be taken as indicative of substantial stress. The average score for the sample was 0.44, and 12% of the respondents had scores above 1.

Days of sickness absence over the last 12 months were also measured. The average number was 6.2, but the distribution was highly skewed, with a mode of zero and a median of 2.0. Therefore log transformation was used to provide a normalised distribution for purposes of analysis. It is possible that actual health and days of sickness absence are not strongly related. It is possible to continue to work despite ill-health and it is possible that employees take sickness absence when they are not actually ill.

Turnover intention was scored on a scale with mean scores from 1 to 7, scores above 4 indicating agreement with the intention to leave the organisation. The average score was 3.95, and 45% scored above the midpoint of 4.

In summary, the sample showed generally low levels of stress, relatively low levels of family–work conflict and very high levels of family–work support. However, they experienced high levels of work–family conflict and had high levels of intention to leave their organisation. The overall picture is one in which the family contributes positively to supporting work, whereas work contributes negatively to increase conflict (see Appendix A6.1).

Effects of gender, caring responsibilities and occupational level on family and work conflict

Men reported higher levels of family–work conflict (mean = 2.56) than women (mean = 2.37). While this is true for managerial and semi-skilled workers, male and female skilled workers had similar scores. Men also reported experiencing more work–family conflict (mean = 4.11) than women (mean = 3.70).

Carers experienced more family–work conflict (mean = 2.66) than non-carers (mean = 2.38), and

more work–family conflict (mean = 4.21) than non-carers (mean = 3.80).

Therefore, overall, managerial and semi-skilled male employees, and carers, experienced more conflicts between family and work than did managerial and semi-skilled women, and non-carers, respectively (see also Appendix A6.2b).

Difficulties caused by work conflicting with family life were also clear from the interview study in which a number of male shop stewards described difficulty in 'switching off' from work pressures once they are at home:

"There's no conflict from home. My wife is very understanding. She knows I get enough grief from work so she's not going to give me any more. She's very supportive and the kids accept my working hours."
(Male shop steward, 39 yrs, production, stated that he had no childcare responsibilities)

"When I am tired because of the shifts, I can take it out on the family." (Male shop steward, 36 yrs, operative, has children)

"It's difficult not to take work problems home. I try to switch off, but it's hard." (Male shop steward, 52 yrs, maintenance electrician, no caring responsibilities)

Effects of age, gender, caring responsibilities and occupational level on number of hours worked, stress, ill-health and turnover intention

The number of hours worked per week was not associated with caring responsibilities and there were only small differences in hours as a function of occupational level or gender. Managers (mean = 39.9) and skilled workers (mean = 39.2) worked slightly longer hours than semi-skilled workers (mean = 38.54). In this sample of full-time workers, men worked just over one hour per week longer than women (means = 39.8 and 38.5 respectively).

Managerial workers had taken fewer days off sick than skilled or semi-skilled workers. Men had taken fewer days off sick than women. This gender difference was especially strong among carers. Male carers and non-carers took a similar number of days off sick (mean log-transformed scores = 0.44, 0.46, respectively), but female carers took substantially more days off (mean = 0.72) than female non-carers (mean = 0.60).

Managers had higher stress (GHQ) scores (mean = 0.68) than skilled or semi-skilled workers (means = 0.32, 0.33, respectively). Moreover, differences in the GHQ scores of these groups were larger for men (means = 0.72, 0.28, 0.27) than women (means = 0.54, 0.39, 0.31, respectively). Thus, male managers show significantly less healthy scores than all other groups. Carers had higher stress scores (mean = 0.48) than non-carers (mean = 0.40).

Turnover intention was not statistically associated with gender, care responsibilities or occupational level (see Appendix A6.3).

In summary, men worked marginally more hours and took marginally fewer days off sick than women, particularly women carers. However, stress was higher among managers, particularly male managers (see Appendix A6.1).

The impact of conflict and flexible working on stress and ill-health

We were particularly interested in whether conflicts between work and family were related to stress, days of sickness absence and turnover intentions, after controlling for the effects of gender, occupational level and caring responsibilities. To test these relationships we used multiple regression. We also examined whether levels of family–work support had any additional effect on health outcomes, and whether number of hours worked and flexible working had any distinct effect. The results of the regression analysis with all variables included are shown in Appendix A6.3.

The results show that psychological responses to the workplace, manifested by GHQ scores and turnover intentions, are both positively related to conflict, but not to hours worked. In contrast, days of sickness absence were positively related to hours worked, but not to conflict variables. GHQ scores, which were notably higher among managerial workers, were also related especially strongly to work–family conflict, and somewhat

less to family–work conflict. In total 19% of the variance in GHQ scores was accounted for. Turnover intention was also most strongly associated with work–family conflict. Perhaps the most surprising finding is that the extent of flexible working does not have any relationship to any of these outcomes, and this would seem to be attributable to the fact that such flexible patterns as do exist are not sufficient to eliminate the effects of conflicts.

We also examined whether GHQ scores mediated the effects of other predictors on days of sickness and turnover intention. GHQ did have significant independent effects on these two outcomes, but did not reduce the effects of the other predictors.

In summary, conflict, particularly from work to family, has adverse consequences both for the psychological health of individuals and for an organisation's capacity to retain its employees.

Flexible working as a possible antecedent to and consequence of conflict

How does the use of, and intention to use, flexible working practices reflect the presence of different types of conflict? To address these questions, we conducted multiple regression analyses to predict current and intended use of flexible working. The predictor variables were, first, age, gender, occupational level and caring responsibility, and, second, work–family conflict, family–work conflict, family–work support and number of hours worked. The results of these analyses are shown in Appendix A6.4.

Current flexible working was negatively associated with work–family conflict but positively related to family–work conflict. This suggests that those using flexible working are doing so as a response to family pressure and that they experience reduced work pressure.

Intention to use flexible working if it is available in future was positively associated with family–work support and work–family conflict, but was not associated with family–work conflict. This suggests that intentions to use flexible working emerge from a combination of support from the family and pressure from work interfering in family life.

The most interesting point to emerge from all this is that work–family conflict has opposite associations with the use of, and intention to use, flexible working. Use of flexible working is related to less work–family conflict, whereas the intention to seek flexible working seems motivated by work–family conflict. Given the previously observed relationship between work–family conflict and turnover intention, it would seem wise for employers to respond to employees' desire for flexible working, as this may reduce work–family conflicts.

Summary

- Respondents showed good psychological health, although stress was higher among men, managers and carers.
- Physical health was also good in general, but women, particularly those with caring responsibilities, had taken slightly more days than men in sick leave.
- Days of sickness absence were affected by number of hours worked but not by conflicts between work and family.
- In this sample of full-time workers, men worked, on average, only one hour more per week than women.
- A large majority of workers experienced support rather than conflict arising from their family's orientation towards their work.
- In contrast, half of the workers experienced conflict at home arising from pressure from their work.
- Work–family conflict is lower among employees who use flexible working, but higher among those who intend to use such arrangements if they become available.
- Almost half of the employees intended to leave their organisation at some point in the future.
- Stress and turnover intention were both affected independently by work–family conflict rather than being directly affected by flexible working practices.

7

The impact of workplace culture on flexible working, conflict and occupational outcomes

In Chapter 6 we examined the personal variables that were related to the use of, and intention to use, flexible working. In this chapter we examine organisational variables – particularly aspects of work–family culture in the workplace. As with our previous analyses, we explore this question while also taking into account employees' gender, caring responsibilities and organisational level. The relationship between workplace culture and personal outcomes – support and conflict in work and family life, stress and turnover intention – are also examined.

The availability of flexible working practices is an essential precondition to their uptake by employees. However, research has shown that the availability of such practices does not necessarily lead to uptake. Thompson et al (1999) and Allen (2001) found that both perceived supervisor support and perceptions of family supportive organisations were positively related to overall use of flexible working arrangements. Guzzo et al (1994) found that family-oriented actions by the organisation served to increase the perceptions of managers that their organisation was supportive. Thompson et al (1999) provided evidence to suggest that the type and number of work–family programmes offered is not as important as the culture of an organisation, which, in itself, is crucial for determining not only whether people will use benefits, but also their general attitudes towards the organisation (Galinsky and Stein, 1990; Lewis and Taylor, 1996; Thompson et al, 1999).

Thompson et al (1999) developed a measure of *work–family culture*. This is the extent to which an organisation supports and values the integration of employees' work and family lives. Thompson et al developed a 20-item scale to measure work–family culture which assesses perceptions of the extent to which the organisation facilitates employees' efforts to balance work and family responsibilities. Using data from 276 managers and professionals, the authors identified three dimensions of work–family culture: the extent to which managers were supportive and sensitive to employees' family responsibilities (*managerial support*); the extent to which there were perceived negative career consequences associated with the use of work–family benefits (*career consequences*); and, finally, the extent to which employees experienced organisational time demands or expectations that might interfere with non-work responsibilities (*organisational time demands*).

It seems reasonable to expect that the use of flexible working practices should be affected by these aspects of workplace culture, as should intentions to adopt such practices. However, a more direct and powerful relationship is likely to exist between the workplace culture and the experience of conflict and support in work and family life, stress and turnover intention. This chapter investigates these questions.

Measures and overall pattern of responses

Work–family culture in the workplace (workplace culture)

Workplace culture was measured using the three subscales designed by Thompson et al (1999) – *managerial support, career consequences* and *organisational time demands*. A fourth scale was devised by us to tap an additional element of workplace culture – the extent to which the union is perceived as supporting family-friendly policies.

All four scales had mean scores which can range from 1 (strongly disagree) to 7 (strongly agree), and a neutral point of 4.

First we examined the distribution of responses and the multivariate effects of age, gender, occupational level and caring responsibilities on responses to the four measures of workplace culture (see Appendix A7.1). All statistically reliable differences are reported below.

Managerial support for family-related needs

Fifty-three per cent of respondents agreed or strongly agreed that managers in their organisation were sensitive and responsive to family and personal issues (mean = 4.04). However, this perception was not shared by all. Managers (mean = 4.25) perceived greater support than skilled (mean = 4.03) or semi-skilled workers (mean = 3.75).

Negative career consequences of family-friendly practices

Forty per cent of respondents agreed that using family-friendly practices would be damaging for their careers (mean = 3.80). In this instance, managers felt family-friendly practices would be more damaging for their careers (mean = 3.98) than did skilled (mean = 3.70) and semi-skilled workers (mean = 3.73).

Organisational time demands

Forty-six per cent of respondents felt that people had to put their work before their family and personal life in order to progress within their organisation (mean = 3.97). Managers again felt that the organisation's time demands were more pressing (mean = 4.20) than did either skilled (mean = 3.88) or semi-skilled workers (mean = 3.78). In addition, men felt that the organisational demands were more pressing (mean = 4.10) than did women (mean = 3.71).

Union support for family-friendly policies

Fifty-six per cent of respondents felt their union recognised and promoted family needs (mean = 4.32). Women felt more supported by their union (mean = 4.40) than did men (mean = 4.27).

There were no differences between carers and non-carers on any of these measures. In summary, managers felt more supported but also more pressured and had greater concern about career prospects than did other groups of workers. Men felt more pressured by organisational demands and also less supported by their union than did women (also see Appendix A7.2a).

How does workplace culture relate to flexible working and intentions to use flexible working?

We conducted multiple regression analyses to predict the extent of current and intended use of flexible working. The predictor variables were, first, gender, occupational level and caring responsibility and, second, the four measures of workplace culture. The results of these analyses are shown in Table 7.1.

There was very little evidence that workplace culture was related to flexible working. Indeed the only statistically significant relationship was that those who currently used flexible working practices perceived greater management support for those practices.

The link between workplace culture and conflict, health and turnover intention

We were particularly interested in how the different aspects of workplace culture would be associated, first, with employees' experience of conflict between work and family and, second, with their health outcomes and turnover intention. To test this we used multiple regression analysis.

The results of the regression analysis with all variables included are shown in Table 7.2.

Table 7:1: The relationship between workplace culture and current and intended use of flexible working practices

Flexible working measure Predictor variables	Current	Intended
Age	0.00	−0.08**
Gender	−0.06*	0.09**
Managerial level	0.12***	0.14***
Semi-skilled level	−0.02	−0.05
Caring responsibilities	0.03	0.04
Management support	0.11***	−0.01
Negative career consequences	−0.01	0.01
Organisational demands	0.00	−0.01
Union support for family-friendly practices	0.03	0.04
R^2	0.04***	0.04***

Note: Non-italicised figures are standardised regression coefficients. Italicised figures are total variance accounted for.
*$p < 0.05$, ** $p<0.01$, *** $p<0.001$.

Table 7.2: Effects of demographic variables and organisational impact on conflict, psychological and physical health and turnover intentions

Outcomes Predictor variables	Family–work conflict	Work–family conflict	Family–work support	GHQ	Days of sickness	Turnover intention
Age	−0.07**	−0.05*	−0.01	−0.02	−0.02	−0.13***
Gender	−0.05	−0.06**	0.02	0.01	0.14***	0.02
Managerial level	0.06**	0.03	0.01	0.32***	−0.15***	0.04
Semi-skilled level	0.01	0.01	−0.02	0.01	0.03	−0.01
Caring responsibilities	0.10***	0.08***	0.04	0.06**	0.03	−0.04
Management support	0.05	−0.18***	0.07*	−0.09**	−0.03	−0.24***
Negative career consequences	0.17***	0.08**	0.04	0.11***	0.03	0.15***
Organisational demands	0.06	0.33***	0.13***	0.08**	0.03	0.03
Union support	−0.07**	−0.03	0.14***	−0.02	−0.01	−0.08**
R^2	0.07***	0.27***	0.04***	0.17***	0.06***	0.15***

Note: Non-italicised figures are standardised regression coefficients. Italicised figures are total variance accounted for.
* $p<0.05$, ** $p<0.01$, *** $p<0.001$.

Employees' family–work conflict was greatest among respondents who perceived negative career consequences of using flexible working, and those who felt their union did not support family-friendly working. However, the more dramatic finding concerns work–family conflict. Those who experienced higher work–family conflict reported lower management support for flexible working, more negative career consequences and, in particular, high levels of organisational demand on their time. A substantial percentage (27%) of the variance in work–family conflict was explained by these organisational impacts.

Employees' experience of stress (GHQ) was also affected by organisational impacts. Higher levels of stress were associated with less management support, negative career consequences and high organisational demands. Interestingly, none of the organisational impact measures were related to days of leave due to sickness.

Intention to leave their organisation was also clearly associated with organisational impacts – specifically, low management support for flexible working, negative career consequences and low union support for family-friendly working.

The picture that emerges is that when employees experience high organisational demands on their time, managers who do not recognise the importance of family time, and a reward structure that appears punitive to those who have non-work commitments, they experience psychological distress and are motivated to leave their organisation.

Summary

- Employees were fairly evenly divided in feeling that their organisation and its management, as well as their union, supported flexible working.
- Managers felt there was more managerial support for flexible working, but they were also more concerned about the career consequences of pursuing flexible working.
- Men felt more organisational pressure and less union support for flexible working practices than did women.
- Management support was associated with greater use of flexible working, but workplace culture as a whole did not directly affect employees' intentions to use flexible working practices.
- A non-supportive workplace culture was associated with higher levels of work–family conflict, poorer psychological health and stronger intentions to leave the organisation.

8

A model of orientation to work and personal life

In the previous chapters we have observed how, once gender, occupational level and caring responsibilities are controlled, attitudes to flexible working are related to whether a person is currently using, and intends to use, flexible working practices. The model presented in Chapter 5 suggested that personal and organisational variables could affect employees' attitudes to flexible working directly, and could also have distinct effects on their actual and intended use of flexible working practices. Subsequently, in Chapters 6 and 7, we operationalised these personal and organisational variables as forms of conflict/support involving work and family, and workplace culture, respectively. We established that conflict predicts use, and intended use, of flexible working practices, and that workplace culture also plays a limited role. We also showed that conflict and workplace culture have other effects, on employees' health and turnover intention.

This chapter will try to complete the model developed in Chapter 5. This requires several further sets of analyses. First, we need to establish whether attitudes to flexible working are linked to work–family conflict and workplace culture. If they are, the question is whether conflict and workplace culture affect employees' use and intended use of flexible working independently of the impact of attitudes, seen in Chapter 5. Three outcomes are possible. The effects of attitudes seen in Chapter 5, and the effects of conflict and culture seen in Chapters 6 and 7, could all occur independently. Alternatively, the effects of conflict and culture could be entirely mediated by attitudes – that is, the effects on flexible working that we observed in Chapters 6 and 7 could be eliminated entirely once the impact of employees' attitudes is statistically accounted for. Finally, it is possible

that conflict and culture have some direct impact on flexible working, and some impact via their relationship with attitudes.

Relationship between conflict and workplace culture and attitudes to flexible working practices

Although we cannot fully test a causal model with our cross-sectional data, it seems reasonable to assume that people develop their attitudes to working practices in the light of their experiences of working. For this reason it also seems conceptually justifiable to consider that workplace culture and conflicts between family and work life probably precede the formation of attitudes to flexible working practices. Therefore we decided to conduct multiple regression analyses to see how the three conflict measures and the four workplace culture measures predicted each of the attitudes to flexible working practices, described in Chapter 5. Because this analysis involves presentation of a large volume of statistics, we have not included the effects of age, gender, occupational level and caring responsibilities in Table 8.1, as these have been reported previously. However, those four predictors were included in the regression prior to all other predictors. Therefore the effects reported in the table are independent of the effects of those demographic variables. The additional variance accounted for by the attitudinal variables is the difference between the R^2 figures in the first and last rows of the table.

Table 8.1: The relationship between work–family conflict and workplace culture, and employees' attitudes to flexible work practices

Attitude	Personal benefits	Employer benefits	Employee success	Engagement	Poor performance	Long hours positive	Long hours negative
R^2 from demographic predictors †	*0.04****	*0.03****	*0.01*	*0.02****	*0.04****	*0.01***	*0.01*
Additional predictors							
Work–family conflict	0.10***	0.03	-0.01	0.09**	0.04	0.03	0.14***
Family–work conflict	-0.14***	-0.04	0.10***	0.01	0.13***	0.08**	-0.06**
Family–work support	0.07**	0.12***	0.04	0.12***	-0.08***	-0.01	0.09***
Manager support	0.07*	0.03	0.25***	0.04	0.11***	0.16***	-0.02
Negative career consequences	0.06*	0.06*	-0.01	0.09**	0.10***	0.06*	0.09**
Organisational demands	-0.01	-0.03	0.04	0.02	0.04	0.19***	0.02
Union support	0.14***	0.08**	0.05	0.05*	-0.09**	0.02	0.06*
Total R^2	*0.09****	*0.06****	*0.08****	*0.07****	*0.09****	*0.07****	*0.06****

Note: † These include age, gender, occupational level and caring responsibilities. Non-italicised figures are standardised regression coefficients. Italicised figures are total variance accounted for. * $p < 0.05$, ** $p < 0.01$, *** $p < 0.001$.

From these analyses it is clear that all seven of the employee attitude measures are affected, in various ways, by the conflict and by the culture variables. The most substantial relationships appear in the case of the perceived personal benefits of flexible working, the expectations for career success and work performance. All three of these attitudes were associated with family–work conflict. More pressure from family on work was linked to the belief that flexible working would result in worse outcomes for the employee. All three attitudes were also related to the level of managerial support for flexible working, the most notable being expectations that flexible working could bring about success at work for the employee. Finally, we note that union support and family support show a similar pattern of effects. Both forms of support are associated with an increased perception that flexible working will bring personal benefits as well as employer benefits, that it will increase engagement with the organisation, that it will not cause poorer work performance, and that long working hours are harmful.

Given that attitudes are related significantly to conflict and workplace culture, it is now important to establish whether each set of variables has a distinct statistical relationship with employees' current use and intended use of flexible working.

In order to assess these final questions we used a path analytic procedure in which we included as predictors in regression analyses only the variables that had significant relationships in prior analyses. Table 8.2 reports the results of a two-stage analytic process. After the effects of the demographic variables are accounted for, the first step in the analysis predicts current and intended use of flexible working from the conflict and culture variables. The second step adds the employee attitude variables to the set of predictors. If an attitude is a significant predictor, and if the regression weight of a conflict or culture variable reduces at this second stage, this provides evidence that the effects of the conflict or culture variable are mediated by the attitude variable.

Table 8.2: The relationship between work–family conflict, workplace culture, employee attitudes and flexible working

Outcome	Flexible working	Intended flexible working
R² from demographic predictors†	*0.02****	*0.03****
Step 1 predictors:		
Work–family conflict	–0.06*	0.07**
Family–work conflict	0.15***	–
Family–work support	0.04	0.10***
Manager support	0.10***	–
R² from demographic plus Step 1 predictors	*0.06****	*0.05****
Step 2 predictors:		
Work–family conflict	–0.05	0.06**
Family–work conflict	0.14***	–
Family–work support	0.01	0.02
Manager support	0.08**	–
Personal benefits	–0.08**	0.23***
Employer benefits	0.13***	0.08**
Employee success	0.10***	–
Engagement	–	0.18***
Poorer performance	–0.07*	–0.22***
Total R²	*0.09****	*0.28****

Note: † These include age, gender and occupational level. Non-italicised figures are standardised regression coefficients. Italicised figures are total variance accounted for. * $p<0.05$, ** $p<0.01$, *** $p<0.001$. Blank lines indicate that the predictor variable did not have a significant relationship with flexible working in the earlier analyses.

These analyses revealed the following statistical relationships. Those employees who used flexible working currently had higher levels of family–work conflict, higher levels of manager support, perceived fewer personal benefits but more employer benefits and chances for success, and anticipated less poor performance. Stronger intentions to use flexible working practices are associated with the presence of work–family conflict. Family–work support also had an effect but this is mediated via attitudes – perceptions that there will be higher personal benefits and employer benefits, higher engagement and the belief that performance will not suffer.

In summary, conflict, culture and attitudes each have distinct associations with employees' current use of flexible working. Conflict and attitudes also have distinct effects on intentions to use flexible working; however, some of the impact of conflict is mediated through employees' attitudes.

Effects of attitudes, conflict and culture on health and turnover intentions

A similar procedure to the previous analysis was pursued to investigate the unique and mediated relationships between work–family conflict, workplace culture and employee attitudes with GHQ scores and turnover intention. Days of sickness leave were not predicted at all by conflict or culture so there was no possibility that effects of these variables could be mediated by attitudes.

In a preliminary analysis we examined which demographic variables and attitudes predicted each of these outcomes significantly. GHQ scores were significantly associated with managerial status ($\beta = 0.30$, $p<0.001$), caring responsibilities ($\beta = 0.07$, $p<0.01$), perceived personal benefits ($\beta = 0.06$, $p<0.05$), lower employee success ($\beta = -0.08$, $p<0.001$) and poorer performance ($\beta = 0.10$, $p<0.001$), R² = 0.13. Employees' turnover intentions were significantly associated with their age ($\beta = -0.12$, $p<0.001$), and with disagreement that long working hours are positive ($\beta = -0.10$, $p<0.001$)

and agreement that long working hours are negative (β = 0.10, $p<0.001$), R^2 = 0.02 (see Appendix A8.1).

The results are shown in Table 8.3. Analysis was in two steps. The first step shows that the demographic, culture and conflict variables are distinctly related to GHQ and to turnover intention. The second step shows whether the attitudes to flexible working explain any additional variance in GHQ and turnover intention once the step 1 variables are accounted for.

The standardised regression coefficients (β values) for the predictors in both step 1 and step 2 of Table 8.3 are almost identical. This indicates that the statistical relationships that GHQ and turnover intention have with conflict and culture are independent of the relationships they have with attitudes. Taken together, these analyses show that conflict, workplace culture and employee attitudes each make a distinct contribution to the variations in their psychological health and turnover intention.

Taken as a whole, the results of the various regression analyses from Chapters 5, 6 and 7 can be depicted schematically in Figure 8.1. This figure represents the relationships among the variables that we measured, in the form of a model of employees' orientation to the relationship between work and personal life.

This model suggests that demographic variables affect people's perceptions of their organisation, their work–home conflicts and their attitudes towards flexible working. Workplace culture and work–home conflicts also affect people's attitudes to flexible working. Workplace culture, conflicts and attitudes can each affect various outcomes. Different elements of these three types of variable affect employees' current flexible working, their intended flexible working, turnover intentions and their psychological health. In contrast, employees' physical health is relatively unaffected by these variables.

As a whole, our evidence shows that demographic variables have some effect on employees' relationship to their working environment. These variables also have associations with whether employees use flexible working and with their psychological health. Organisational variables and personal variables

Table 8.3: Effects of demographic variables, work–family conflict, workplace culture and attitudes on psychological health and turnover intention

Outcome	GHQ	Turnover intention
Predictors Step 1:		
Age	–	–0.12***
Managerial level	0.29***	–
Caring responsibilities	0.03	–
Work–family conflict	0.18***	0.08**
Family–work conflict	0.09***	–
Family–work support	–0.04	–
Manager support	–0.08**	–0.22***
Negative career consequences	0.07**	0.14***
Organisational demands	0.02	–
Union support	–	–0.08***
R^2 from step 1 predictors	*0.19***	*0.15****
Step 2:		
Age	–	–0.13***
Managerial level	0.29***	–
Caring responsibilities	0.03	–
Work–family conflict	0.17***	0.09***
Family–work conflict	0.10***	–
Family–work support	–0.03	–
Manager support	–0.07**	–0.21***
Negative career consequences	0.06*	0.15***
Organisational demands	0.02	–
Union support	–	–0.08***
Personal benefits	0.06**	–
Employee success	–0.05*	–
Poorer performance	0.04	–
Long hours positive	–	–0.11***
Long hours negative	–	0.05*
Total R^2	*0.20***	*0.16****

Note: Non-italicised figures are standardised regression coefficients. Italicised figures are total variance accounted for. * $p<0.05$, ** $p<0.01$, *** $p<0.001$

(workplace culture and work–family conflict) both influence attitudes to flexible work practices. Together, the three sets of variables (culture, conflict and attitudes) affect employees' flexible working intentions, their turnover intentions and their psychological health. The findings presented in this report can now be summarised in the context of our model.

Figure 8:1: A model of orientation to work and personal life

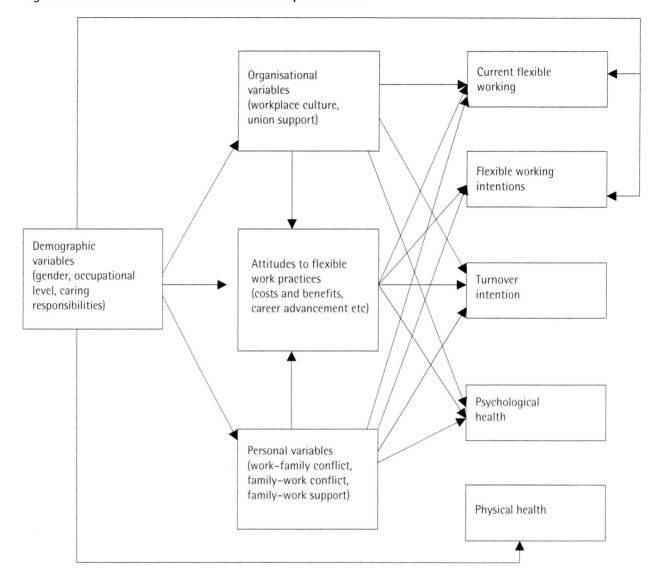

Note: Arrows represent independent statistically significant relationships.

Summary of findings in relation to the model

Effects of gender, occupational level and caring responsibilities

The men in our sample had a more negative attitude towards flexible working, in terms of personal benefits, employer benefits, and the extent to which it would bring engagement with the organisation and produce poor work performance. The male employees experienced slightly higher levels of work–family conflict. Men felt that organisational demands were more pressing and that their union was less supportive of family-friendly policies than women did. Women were more likely to take days off sick,

but women and men did not differ in their psychological health or turnover intentions. Although men and women were equally likely to use flexible working, women were more likely to intend to use flexible working practices if they became available to them.

Managers had a more positive attitude towards flexible working than other employees, but experienced slightly more family–work conflict. Managers felt that the organisation made greater demands on their time, and that family-friendly policies were more damaging to their careers, than did other workers. Managerial workers experienced worse psychological health, and had slightly higher turnover intentions, but took fewer days off sick compared with less senior workers. Despite all this, managers were more likely to use, and intend to use, flexible working practices.

Carers were more likely to consider that flexible working improved engagement with the organisation. In other respects they did not differ from non-carers in their attitudes to, or use of, flexible working. Carers and non-carers had similar views of workplace culture. However, carers had more work–family conflict and more family–work conflict than non-carers, and slightly worse psychological health.

Likely effects of workplace culture and conflict on employees' attitudes to flexible working

Employees' attitudes to flexible working were substantially linked to workplace culture and conflicts. Those who experienced conflict from family pressures were more likely to believe that flexible working would result in negative career outcomes. Employees' attitudes to flexible working were more negative if they perceived lower levels of managerial support. In contrast, employees who had greater union support and family support for flexible working practices held more positive expectations that flexible working would benefit employees and employer alike.

Likely effects of workplace culture, work–family conflict and employee attitudes on other outcomes

Employees who used flexible working had more supportive managers, lower work–family conflict and expected that flexible working practices would bring benefits for employees and employers. Employees had stronger intentions to use flexible working in future if they felt flexible working would bring personal benefits, that it would not lead to poor work performance and if they had higher levels of family support.

Employees' psychological health was worsened if they experienced more work–family and family–work conflict, lower managerial support for flexible working, and worked in a culture which was negative about flexible working.

Employees had stronger intentions to leave the organisation if they experienced more work–family conflict and lower manager and union support for flexible working practices.

Summary

- A model of orientation to work and personal life suggests that demographic factors influence perceptions of organisational variables, attitudes to flexible work and personal variables. These in turn are linked to use of flexible working practices, turnover intention and psychological health.
- Positive attitudes to flexible working are associated with less conflict between work and family life, and a more positive work–family culture in the workplace.
- Lower work–family conflict, more positive workplace culture and more positive attitudes to flexible working practices are all associated with employees' greater use of flexible working.
- Higher levels of work–family conflict and a more negative workplace culture are associated with poorer psychological health for employees and a stronger intention to leave their organisation.

9

Conclusions and implications for policy

Our interview study revealed a proportion of shop stewards – skilled workers in traditional male employment contexts – who regarded flexible working with either misunderstanding or mistrust. There was clear anxiety that traditional patterns of work, particularly shift working and overtime, would be threatened by flexible working. The interview study enabled us to explore some quite negative attitudes to changes in traditional work and family patterns, and to women and work, which might not have come to light in the questionnaire survey.

The views held by the shop stewards we interviewed can be contrasted with the results from the questionnaire study in relation to preferred patterns of work and family life. Overall the most strongly preferred option for work and family life was for both parents to work flexibly and to share childcare and work in the home. Thus while there are clearly a proportion of men who are anxious about changes in working patterns, there is also growing recognition that family life might be better if men and women were able to share work and family responsibilities more evenly.

In general we discovered a preference for the term 'flexible' rather than 'family-friendly' when describing patterns of work designed to improve work–life balance. Our respondents also showed stronger preferences for general employment benefits – pensions, extra holiday entitlement and health insurance – than for policies that provided flexibility in working hours or locations. However, women, and those with any kind of caring responsibility, were more strongly in favour of flexible working and rights for working parents.

The respondents in our questionnaire survey were full-time workers and within this sample fewer women than men claimed to have caring responsibilities. However, those women who did have caring responsibilities devoted double the amount of time to them than the men who reported also having caring responsibilities. Thus the experience of work–life balance among full-time workers with caring responsibilities may be very different depending on gender.

Among our respondents, male managers were most likely, and female semi-skilled workers least likely, to be current users of flexible working practices. However, the majority of respondents (72%) intended to use flexible working if it became possible in the future – women more so than men, and managers more so than skilled or semi-skilled workers.

The women who took part in our survey felt more positively about flexible working than men. Among both men and women there were strong expectations that flexible working would be good for the employer and employee, particularly among women and managerial workers. However, the majority also disagreed that flexible working would lead to respect and promotion for employees who used it.

Employees' attitudes were strongly associated with their intentions to use flexible working. Workers who perceived greater personal benefits, better engagement with the organisation and fewer negative work outcomes were those who expressed the strongest intention to use flexible working practices if they became available to them.

When asked about the relationship between their working and family lives, the majority of our respondents experienced support rather than conflict arising from their family's orientation towards their work. In contrast, half of the workers experienced conflict at home arising from pressure from their work. Work–family conflict is lower among employees who use flexible working, but higher among those who intend to use it if it becomes available. Experience of stress and intention to leave current employment were both affected independently by work–family conflict rather than being directly affected by flexible working practices.

Respondents were fairly evenly divided in their views about whether their organisation and its management, as well as their union, supported flexible working. Managers felt more supported than other employees, but they were also more concerned about the career consequences of pursuing flexible working. Men felt a higher level of organisational demands than women, and that there was less union support for flexible working practices. Management support for flexible working arrangements was associated with greater use of flexible working, but workplace culture as a whole did not directly affect intentions to use flexible working practices. A non-supportive workplace culture was associated with higher levels of work–family conflict, poorer psychological health and stronger intentions to leave the organisation.

Our suggested model of orientation to work and personal life suggests that demographic factors influence employees' perceptions of organisational variables, their attitudes to flexible work and personal variables. These in turn are linked to employees' use of flexible working practices, their turnover intentions and their psychological health. Positive attitudes to flexible working were associated with less conflict between work and family life, and a more positive work–family culture in the workplace. Lower conflict, more positive workplace culture and more positive attitudes to flexible working practices were all associated with greater use of flexible working. Higher levels of conflict and a more negative workplace culture are associated with poorer psychological health and a stronger intention to leave the organisation.

Our research has shown that very traditional views about work and family life prevail among some men in male-dominated employment sectors. Despite this there is an overall preference for families to combine work and family life more equally, and a strong preference to use flexible working practices if they become available. Our findings indicate that arrangements that are available to the entire workforce will be more easily accepted than those aimed at particular groups such as carers. Women and those in management are likely to lead the way in uptake of more flexible ways of working. Men may also feel that they would like greater equality in work and caring, but are more likely to see barriers to this within their job. The implications of this are that flexible working arrangements will need greater promotion among male workers and more will have to be done to establish that flexible working does not necessarily mean poor career prospects. Moreover, if more men and women are to be able to find a more equal division of work and caring then continued efforts need to be made to facilitate women's participation in the workforce.

There is some evidence for a business case for flexible working arrangements (Dex and Scheibl, 2002). Our research shows that flexible working is related to commitment to remain with a current employer and has a positive impact on both psychological health and family life.

References

Abrams, D., Ando, K. and Hinkle, S. (1998) 'Psychological attachment to the group: cross cultural differences in organizational identification and subjective norms as predictors of workers' turnover intentions', *Personality and Social Psychology Bulletin*, vol 10, pp 1027-39.

Allen, T.D. (2001) 'Family-supportive work environments: the role of organizational perceptions', *Journal of Vocational Behavior*, vol 58, pp 414-35.

Belsky, J. (1990) 'Parental and nonparental child care and children's socioemotional development: a decade in review', *Journal of Marriage and the Family*, vol 52, pp 885-903.

Brandth, B. and Kvande, E. (2001) 'Flexible work and flexible fathers', *Work, Employment and Society*, vol 15, no 2, pp 251-67.

Cook, A.H. (1992) 'Can work requirements accommodate to the needs of dual-earner families?', in S. Lewis, D.N. Izraeli and H. Hootsman (eds) *Dual-earner families: International perspectives*, London: Sage Publications, pp 204-20.

Cox, T. (1978) *Stress*, London: Macmillan.

Dex, S. (1999) *Families and the labour market: Trends, pressures and policies*, York: Joseph Rowntree Foundation.

Dex, S. and Scheibl, F. (2002) *SMEs and flexible working arrangements*, Bristol/York: The Policy Press/Joseph Rowntree Foundation.

Dex, S. and Smith, C. (2002) *The nature and pattern of family-friendly employment policies in Britain*, Family and Work Series, Bristol/York: The Policy Press/Joseph Rowntree Foundation.

DfEE (Department for Education and Employment) (2000) *Worklife balance: Changing patterns in a changing world*, London: The Stationery Office.

Duxbury, L., Higgins, C., Lee, C. and Mills, S. (1991) *Balancing work and family: A study of the Canadian federal public sector*, prepared for the Department of Health and Welfare Canada, Ottawa: NHRDP.

Eagle, B.W., Icenogle, M.L., Maes, J.D. and Miles, E.W. (1998) 'The importance of employee demographic profiles for understanding experiences of work–family interrole conflicts', *Journal of Social Psychology*, vol 138, pp 690-709.

Eurostat (2000) *European labour force survey*, Luxembourg: Office for Official Publications for the European Communities.

Friedman, D.E. and Galinsky, E. (1992) 'Work and family issues: a legitimate business concern', in S. Zedeck (ed) *Work, families, and organisations*, San Francisco, CA: Jossey-Bass, pp 168-207.

Frone, M.R., Barnes, G. and Farrell, M. (1994) 'Relationship of work/family conflict to substance abuse among employed mothers: examining the mediating role of negative affect', *Journal of Marriage and the Family*, vol 56, pp 1019-30.

Frone, M.R., Russell, M. and Cooper, M.L. (1992) 'Prevalence of work–family conflict: are work and family boundaries asymmetrically permeable?', *Journal of Organisational Behaviour*, vol 13, pp 723-9.

Galinsky, E. and Stein, P.J. (1990) 'The impact of human resource policies on employees', *Journal of Family Issues*, vol 11, pp 368-83.

Galinsky, E., Bond, J.T. and Friedman, D.E. (1993) *Highlights: The national study of the changing workforce*, New York, NY: Families and Work Institute.

Goldberg, D. and Hillier, V.F. (1979) 'A scaled version of the General Health Questionnaire', *Psychological Medicine*, vol 9, pp 139-45.

Goodstein, J.D. (1994) 'Institutional pressures and strategic responsiveness: employer involvement in work–family issues', *Academy of Management Journal*, vol 37, pp 350-82.

Googins, B.K. (1991) *Work/family conflicts: Private lives – public responses*, New York, NY: Auburn House.

Greenhaus, J. and Beutell, N. (1985) 'Sources of conflict between work and family roles', *Academy of Management Review*, vol 10, pp 76-88.

Guelzow, M.G., Bird, G.W. and Koball, E.H. (1991) 'An exploratory path analysis of the stress process for dual-career men and women', *Journal of Marriage and the Family*, vol 53, pp 151-64.

Gutek, B.A., Repetti, R. and Silver, D. (1988) 'Nonwork roles and stress at work', in C. Cooper and R. Payne (eds) *Causes, coping, and consequences of stress at work* (2nd edn), New York, NY: Wiley, pp 141-74.

Gutek, B.A., Searle, S. and Klepa, L. (1991) 'Rational versus gender role explanations for work–family conflict', *Journal of Applied Psychology*, vol 76, pp 560-8.

Guzzo, R.A., Noonan, K.A. and Elron, E. (1994) 'Expatriate managers and the psychological contract', *Journal of Applied Psychology*, vol 79, pp 617-26.

Hakim, C. (2000) *Work–lifestyle choices in the 21st century*, Oxford: Oxford University Press.

Hellman, C.M. (1997) 'Job satisfaction and intent to leave', *Journal of Social Psychology*, vol 137, pp 677-89.

Hogarth, T., Hasluck, C., Pierre, G., Winterbotham, M. and Vivian, D. (2000) *Work–life balance 2000: Baseline study of work–life balance practices in Great Britain*, London: DfEE.

Judge, T.A., Boudreau, J.W. and Bretz, R.D. (1994) 'Job and life attitudes of male executives', *Journal of Applied Psychology*, vol 79, pp 767-82.

Kahn, R.L., Wolfe, D.M., Quinn, R., Snoek, J.D. and Rosenthal, R.A. (1964) *Organizational stress: Studies in role conflict and ambiguity*, New York, NY: John Wiley and Sons.

Karasek, R.A. (1979) 'Job demands, job decision latitude, and mental strain: implications for job redesign', *Administrative Science Quarterly*, vol 24, pp 285-308.

Kvande, E. (1999) 'Flexible fathers in flexible work organizations', Paper presented at the First Nordic–UK Collaborative Seminar on Gender and Labour Market, Stockholm, May.

Lewis, S. (1992) 'Work and families in the United Kingdom', in S. Zedeck (ed) *Work, families, and organizations*, San Francisco, CA: Jossey-Bass, pp 395-431.

Lewis, S. and Taylor, K. (1996) 'Evaluating the impact of family-friendly employer policies: a case study', in S. Lewis and J. Lewis (eds) *The work–family challenge: Rethinking employment*, London: Sage Publications, pp 112-27.

Lloyd, K. (2000) 'Attitudes towards flexible working: a British survey', unpublished MSc dissertation, University of Kent.

Major, B. (1993) 'Gender, entitlement, and the distribution of family labor', *Journal of Social Issues*, vol 49, pp 141-59.

Netemeyer, R.G., Boles, J.S. and McMurrian, R. (1996) 'Development and validation of work–family conflict and family–work conflict scales', *Journal of Applied Psychology*, vol 81, pp 400-10.

ONS (Office for National Statistics) (2001) *Labour force survey*, London: ONS, Spring.

Parcel, T.L. and Menaghan, E.G. (1994) *Parents' jobs and children's lives*, New York, NY: Aldine De Gruyter.

Perlow, L.A. (1995) 'Putting the work back into work/family', *Group and Organisational Management*, vol 20, pp 227-39.

Piotrkowski, C.S., Rapoport, R.N. and Rapoport, R. (1987) 'Families and work', in M.B. Sussman and S.K. Steinmetz (eds) *Handbook of marriage and the family*, New York, NY: Plenum, pp 251-79.

Pleck, J.H. (1985) *Working wives/working husbands*, Newbury Park, CA: Sage Publications.

Powell, G.N. (1997) 'The sex difference in employee inclinations regarding work–family programs: why does it exist, should we care, and what should be done about it (if anything)?', in S. Parasuraman and J.H. Greenhaus (eds) *Integrating work and family: Challenges and choices for a changing world*, Westport, CT: Quorum, pp 167-74.

Powell, G.N. and Mainiero, L.A. (1999) 'Managerial decision making regarding alternative work arrangements', *Journal of Occupational and Organizational Psychology*, vol 72, pp 41-56.

Purcell, K., Hogarth, T. and Simm, C. (1999) *Whose flexibility? The costs and benefits of 'non-standard' working arrangements and contractual relations*, York: Joseph Rowntree Foundation.

Repetti, R.L. (1994) 'Short-term and long-term processes linking job stressors to father–child interaction', *Social Development*, vol 3, pp 1-15.

Repetti, R.L. and Wood, J. (1997) 'Effects of daily stress at work on mothers' interactions with preschoolers', *Journal of Family Psychology*, vol 11, pp 90-108.

Reynolds, T., Callender, C. and Edwards, R. (2003) *Caring and counting: The impact of mothers' employment on family relationships*, Bristol/York: The Policy Press/Joseph Rowntree Foundation.

Sandqvist, K. (1992) 'Sweden's sex-role scheme and commitment to gender equality', in S. Lewis, D.N. Izraeli and H. Hootsmans (eds) *Dual-earner families: International perspectives*, London: Sage Publications, pp 80-98.

Statistics Norway (2001) Grunntabeller: Arbeidskraftundersøkelsen (AKU/LFS) Seksjon for arbeidsmavkedsstatistikk.

Steel, R.P. and Ovalle, N.K. (1984) 'A review and meta-analysis of research on the relationship between behavioural intentions and employee turnover', *Journal of Applied Psychology*, vol 69, pp 673-86.

Stewart, W. and Barling, J. (1996) 'Fathers' work experiences affect children's behaviours via job-related affect and parenting behaviours', *Journal of Organizational Behaviour*, vol 17, pp 221-32.

Thompson, C.A., Beauvais, L.L. and Lyness, K.S. (1999) 'When work–family benefits are not enough: the influence of work–family culture on benefit utilization, organizational attachment, and work–family conflict', *Journal of Vocational Behavior*, vol 54, pp 392-415.

Warin, J., Solomon, Y., Lewis, C. and Langford, W. (1999) *Fathers, work and family life*, York: Joseph Rowntree Foundation.

Yeandle, S., Wigfield, A., Crompton, R. and Dennett, J. (2002) *Employed carers, communities and family-friendly employment policies*, Family and Work Series, Bristol/York: The Policy Press/Joseph Rowntree Foundation.

Appendix A: Statistics

Chapter 2

A2.1: Mean, standard deviation and Cronbach's alpha (reliability) coefficients for the multiple item scales

Name of measure	Mean	Standard deviation	Cronbach's alpha
Intention to use flexible working	5.47	1.63	0.69
Personal benefits	5.81	1.24	0.72
Employee success	3.61	1.33	0.73
Engagement	4.54	1.39	0.74
Poor performance	3.00	1.19	0.70
Positive aspects of long hours	3.65	1.44	0.61
Negative aspects of long hours	5.60	1.30	0.65
Work–family conflict	3.96	1.65	0.89
Family–work conflict	2.49	1.19	0.80
Managerial support	4.04	1.07	0.87
Negative career consequences	4.20	1.17	0.70
Organisational time demands	4.03	1.48	0.74
Family–work support	4.46	1.32	0.82
Union support	4.32	1.35	0.87
Stress (GHQ)	0.44	0.53	0.94
Turnover intention	3.94	1.88	0.78

Note: Scores may range from 1 to 7 for all scales except the GHQ, for which the range is 0-3. Alpha coefficients range from 0 (no reliability) to 1 (100% reliability). The higher the number, the less statistical error there will be in the measurement provided by the scale.

Chapter 4

A4.1: Multivariate and univariate ANOVA statistics for the effects of age, gender, occupational level and caring responsibilities on approval of employment rights and benefits

Benefits	Age (covariate)	Gender	Level	Carer	Gender x Level	Gender x Carer	Level x Carer	Gender x Level x Carer
Multivariate effect	6.74*** (-)	4.92***	3.08***	1.75**	0.81	1.18	0.82	0.99
Univariate effects (1,136df)								
Statutory								
Maternity leave	5.12* (-)	22.26***	6.14**	12.70***	1.16	0.31	3.21*	0.04
Paternity leave (unpaid)	7.51** (-)	2.09	14.27***	0.26	0.02	0.09	0.96	0.45
Parental leave	12.72*** (-)	1.92	4.02*	11.99***	0.11	0.01	0.20	0.84
Non-statutory								
Extra maternity leave over and above statutory requirements	39.94*** (-)	9.11**	5.75**	14.51***	0.12	0.88	1.07	0.49
Paternity leave (paid)	40.82*** (-)	1.73	6.00**	12.81***	0.28	0.02	0.09	0.78
Childcare vouchers or subsidy	5.57* (-)	4.46*	5.96**	12.18***	3.34*	2.51	0.36	0.77
Workplace nursery	0.72	13.14***	8.63***	5.93**	0.34	3.66	0.61	0.08
Posts which are part-time	0.01	29.81***	10.91***	0.61	1.44	0.67	0.46	0.92
Opportunity to switch from full-time to part-time work	3.26	28.31***	3.89*	0.35	0.64	0.09	0.31	1.83
Opportunity to switch from part-time to full-time work	4.88** (+)	16.74***	2.44	0.36	1.13	0.93	0.65	1.42
Job-share	0.01	37.65***	5.28**	2.00	0.86	3.78	0.49	0.79
School term-time only contracts	0.01	14.28***	1.81	9.40**	0.71	2.55	2.72	0.17
Choice of whether to do overtime	1.58	0.16	3.75*	0.33	1.36	0.68	0.62	0.86
Flexitime	0.01	4.44*	14.23***	1.22	0.24	1.13	0.05	0.69
Compressed hours of working (working longer, but fewer days)	11.05*** (-)	1.54	5.52***	0.01	2.29	3.08	0.08	0.80
Choice of whether to do shift work	5.13* (-)	0.36	0.06	3.79	0.24	0.09	1.30	0.81
Working at home	0.50	0.02	15.03***	0.97	0.84	0.19	0.25	0.13
Time off for emergencies within the family (paid)	0.15	0.84	2.05	0.93	0.36	0.65	0.11	0.07
Time off for emergencies within the family (unpaid)	1.17	2.70	4.35*	1.84	0.48	0.35	1.38	1.23
Unpaid career break	5.40* (-)	1.92	4.02*	7.01**	0.76	0.62	0.65	2.09
Paid career break	1.05	3.80	10.97***	8.90**	0.60	2.21	0.72	0.05
Health-related insurance	3.66	7.02**	3.05*	0.03	0.18	0.55	0.15	0.76
Financial/share options	0.15	0.75	4.83*	0.03	0.69	0.79	0.02	3.44*
Company car	12.59*** (-)	0.44	8.11***	0.43	0.34	3.42	0.36	0.92
Contributory pension scheme	0.07	0.36	1.92	0.07	1.03	0.17	0.28	2.81
Non-contributory pension scheme	13.75*** (+)	6.00*	9.62***	1.91	0.11	0.76	0.43	0.56
Extra holiday entitlement	0.11	0.60	2.84	0.80	0.17	1.53	0.31	0.03
Retail vouchers	4.18* (-)	1.14	0.73	1.83	0.34	0.07	1.73	0.18

Note: Listwise deletion was used for missing data; that is, data were only included in this analysis for participants who completed all 28 items. * $p<0.05$, ** $p<0.01$, *** $p<0.001$. Where the effect of age is significant, the direction of the relationship is shown in brackets. + indicates that scores on the item become higher with increasing age, - indicates that scores on the item become lower with increasing age.

A4.2: Means and standard deviations of approval ratings of employment rights and benefits as a function of gender, occupational level and caring responsibilities

Benefits	Men (1,002)	Women (507)	Managerial (516)	Skilled (703)	Semi-skilled (288)	Non-carer	Carer	Overall mean
Statutory								
20. Maternity leave	5.83 (1.56)	6.14 (1.43)	6.03 (1.33)	5.91 (1.58)	5.82 (1.68)	5.83 (1.60)	6.08 (1.40)	5.93 (1.53)
23. Paternity leave (unpaid)	4.11 (2.11)	4.06 (2.25)	4.63 (1.96)	3.81 (2.22)	3.81 (2.17)	4.04 (2.16)	4.17 (2.16)	4.09 (2.16)
17. Parental leave	5.41 (1.69)	5.39 (1.89)	5.62 (1.50)	5.33 (1.85)	5.24 (1.94)	5.25 (1.82)	5.62 (1.66)	5.40 (1.77)
Non-statutory								
21. Extra maternity leave over and above statutory requirements	5.09 (1.82)	5.34 (1.91)	5.36 (1.63)	5.15 (1.88)	4.91 (2.10)	5.03 (1.93)	5.39 (1.71)	5.18 (1.86)
22. Paternity leave (paid)	5.51 (1.80)	5.52 (1.95)	5.71 (1.58)	5.48 (1.91)	5.24 (2.09)	5.34 (1.85)	5.75 (1.67)	5.51 (1.85)
1. Childcare vouchers or subsidy	4.71 (1.99)	4.73 (2.21)	4.90 (1.78)	4.70 (2.02)	4.43 (2.23)	4.62 (1.99)	4.84 (1.98)	4.72 (1.99)
2. Workplace nursery	4.98 (1.91)	5.20 (2.24)	5.37 (1.67)	4.91 (2.12)	4.84 (2.31)	4.98 (2.06)	5.15 (1.99)	4.04 (2.03)
3. Posts which are part-time	4.93 (1.74)	5.39 (1.98)	5.35 (1.52)	5.00 (1.88)	4.85 (2.17)	5.11 (1.81)	5.04 (1.88)	5.08 (1.84)
4. Opportunity to switch from full-time to part-time work	5.04 (1.74)	5.51 (1.98)	5.36 (1.52)	5.11 (1.91)	5.14 (2.14)	5.25 (1.78)	5.12 (1.93)	5.20 (1.84)
5. Opportunity to switch from part-time to full-time work	5.18 (1.67)	5.56 (1.91)	5.45 (1.47)	5.24 (1.83)	5.24 (2.04)	5.34 (1.73)	5.25 (1.81)	5.31 (1.77)
6. Job-share	4.37 (1.90)	4.94 (2.14)	4.76 (1.76)	4.48 (2.06)	4.44 (2.22)	4.55 (1.98)	4.58 (2.03)	4.56 (2.00)
7. School term-time only contracts	4.18 (1.94)	4.44 (2.25)	4.36 (1.86)	4.27 (2.11)	4.08 (2.24)	4.20 (2.03)	4.34 (2.08)	4.26 (2.05)
8. Choice of whether to do overtime	5.78 (1.55)	5.77 (1.66)	5.57 (1.56)	5.89 (1.60)	5.89 (1.59)	5.78 (1.60)	5.79 (1.60)	5.79 (1.59)
10. Flexitime	5.16 (1.77)	5.05 (2.19)	5.53 (1.59)	5.03 (1.91)	4.62 (2.30)	5.09 (1.94)	5.16 (1.90)	5.12 (1.93)

Table A4.2 contd .../

A4.2: contd.../

Benefits	Men (1,002)	Women (507)	Managerial (516)	Skilled (703)	Semi-skilled (288)	Non-carer	Carer	Overall mean
11. Compressed hours of working (working longer, but fewer days)	4.72 (1.89)	4.55 (2.10)	4.87 (1.75)	4.70 (1.98)	4.24 (2.19)	4.70 (1.96)	4.65 (1.97)	4.66 (1.96)
12. Choice of whether to do shift work	4.88 (1.86)	4.72 (2.15)	4.84 (1.72)	4.85 (2.00)	4.76 (2.25)	4.81 (2.00)	4.85 (1.91)	4.82 (1.96)
14. Working at home	4.39 (1.95)	4.16 (2.18)	4.86 (1.74)	4.12 (2.09)	3.80 (2.16)	4.28 (2.06)	4.37 (1.99)	4.31 (2.03)
15. Time off for emergencies within the family (paid)	5.95 (1.54)	5.66 (1.92)	5.91 (1.39)	5.93 (1.68)	5.58 (2.05)	5.79 (1.75)	5.94 (1.58)	5.85 (1.68)
16. Time off for emergencies within the family (unpaid)	4.24 (2.21)	4.42 (2.28)	4.67 (1.99)	4.11 (2.34)	4.14 (2.31)	4.26 (2.25)	4.35 (2.23)	4.30 (2.24)
18. Unpaid career break	4.39 (1.94)	4.37 (2.14)	4.80 (1.79)	4.22 (2.04)	4.07 (2.14)	4.34 (2.06)	4.45 (1.93)	4.38 (2.01)
19. Paid career break	4.74 (2.06)	4.38 (2.23)	4.86 (1.94)	4.60 (2.16)	4.23 (2.29)	4.49 (2.18)	4.80 (2.03)	4.62 (2.12)
24. Health-related insurance	5.66 (1.63)	5.28 (1.98)	5.75 (1.45)	5.53 (1.81)	5.15 (2.06)	5.52 (1.76)	5.36 (1.77)	5.53 (1.76)
25. Financial/share options	5.50 (1.67)	5.23 (1.88)	5.69 (1.46)	5.36 (1.82)	5.04 (1.96)	5.40 (1.76)	5.42 (1.72)	5.41 (1.75)
26. Company car	4.47 (1.89)	4.22 (2.10)	4.79 (1.74)	4.33 (1.98)	3.81 (2.16)	4.35 (2.01)	4.43 (1.90)	4.38 (1.96)
27. Contributory pension scheme	6.19 (1.33)	6.18 (1.45)	6.31 (1.13)	6.14 (1.46)	6.10 (1.52)	6.17 (1.40)	6.22 (1.34)	6.19 (1.37)
28. Non-contributory pension scheme	5.13 (2.07)	4.49 (2.22)	5.28 (1.97)	4.87 (2.18)	4.34 (2.26)	4.87 (2.16)	4.99 (2.12)	4.92 (2.14)
29. Extra holiday entitlement	5.85 (1.59)	5.53 (2.01)	5.85 (1.45)	5.81 (1.74)	5.37 (2.16)	5.70 (1.77)	5.79 (1.71)	5.74 (1.75)
30. Retail vouchers	4.43 (1.92)	4.51 (2.17)	4.35 (1.83)	4.57 (2.02)	4.41 (2.25)	4.44 (1.99)	4.50 (2.02)	4.46 (2.00)

Note: All items are scored from 1 (very poor practice) to 7 (very good practice).

A4.3: Respondents stating that each employment benefit or flexible working opportunity was good (over 4 on a 7-point scale ranging from 1 = very poor practice to 7 = very good practice) (%)

Benefits	Men	Women	Managerial	Skilled	Semi-skilled	Non-carer	Carer	Overall %
Statutory								
20. Maternity leave	81.4	85.6*	86.2	82.1	78.5*	79.2	88.1***	82.8
23. Paternity leave (unpaid)	45.4	43.9	56.4	39.8	35.9***	43.0	47.4	44.8
17. Parental leave	71.9	70.1	76.9	69.5	66.2**	67.5	76.9***	71.3
Non-statutory								
21. Extra maternity leave over and above statutory requirements	65.5	69.6	71.8	66.1	60.1**	62.3	73.8***	67.0
22. Paternity leave (paid)	74.7	72.8	79.1	73.7	65.7***	69.6	80.7***	74.1
1. Childcare vouchers or subsidy	56.1	57.2	59.8	56.9	49.7*	54.7	59.1	56.5
2. Workplace nursery	64.6	70.5*	74.0	63.3	62.2***	65.5	68.4	66.7
3. Posts which are part-time	63.9	73.8***	73.8	64.9	62.4***	68.3	65.9	67.3
4. Opportunity to switch from full-time to part-time work	66.9	75.1***	76.1	66.1	67.5***	70.0	69.1	69.6
5. Opportunity to switch from part-time to full-time work	70.8	76.3*	79.1	69.7	69.0***	72.9	72.2	72.6
6. Job-share	49.5	64.5***	59.6	52.5	51.2*	54.0	55.6	54.6
7. School term-time only contracts	44.3	51.4**	49.3	47.0	42.7	44.7	49.8*	46.8
8. Choice of whether to do overtime	82.8	80.7	80.5	83.2	82.5	81.8	82.9	82.2
10. Flexitime	68.1	65.6	78.3	63.7	56.3***	65.9	69.0	67.1
11. Compressed hours of working (working longer, but fewer days)	60.4	55.9	64.7	59.2	48.3***	58.6	59.5	58.9
12. Choice of whether to do shift work	60.9	57.3	61.6	59.9	56.3	59.1	60.6	59.7
14. Working at home	50.3	45.5	61.8	43.9	36.1***	46.8	51.3	48.6
15. Time off for emergencies within the family (paid)	85.1	79.3**	86.5	83.6	76.8**	81.7	85.3	83.1
16. Time off for emergencies within the family (unpaid)	50.1	53.0	58.3	47.5	47.6***	50.0	52.8	51.1
18. Unpaid career break	48.2	47.2	59.0	43.3	38.8***	46.8	49.4	47.8
19. Paid career break	56.3	48.1**	60.5	52.5	44.1***	51.2	57.4*	53.7
24. Health-related insurance	79.9	70.9***	81.9	77.4	66.7***	76.8	76.9	76.9
25. Financial/share options	76.5	68.7***	81.9	72.8	62.1***	73.5	74.5	73.9
26. Company car	49.5	46.2	57.9	46.7	36.3***	48.7	48.0	48.4
27. Contributory pension scheme	89.0	87.1	91.7	86.7	85.9**	87.4	89.7	88.3
28. Non-contributory pension scheme	65.7	51.4***	69.6	60.5	46.3***	59.9	62.7	61.1
29. Extra holiday entitlement	83.0	75.6***	84.2	81.2	72.0***	79.7	81.7	80.5
30. Retail vouchers	46.6	51.4	43.1	50.8	51.4*	46.4	51.1	48.3

Note: Asterisks indicate significant differences in percentages between comparable groups (that is, gender difference, occupation difference or caring difference). * $p<0.05$, ** $p<0.01$, *** $p<0.001$ by chi square statistics.

A4.4: Rights and benefits rank ordered in terms of percentage of respondents who felt each employment benefit or flexible working opportunity was positive

Rights and benefits	% positive
Contributory pension scheme	88.3
Time off for emergencies within the family (paid)	83.1
Maternity leave	82.8
Choice of whether to do overtime	82.2
Extra holiday entitlement	80.5
Health-related insurance	76.9
Paternity leave (paid)	74.1
Financial/share options	73.9
Opportunity to switch from part-time to full-time work	72.6
Parental leave	71.3
Opportunity to switch from full-time to part-time work	69.6
Posts which are part-time	67.3
Flexitime	67.1
Extra maternity leave over and above statutory requirements	67.0
Workplace nursery	66.7
Non-contributory pension scheme	61.1
Choice of whether to do shift work	59.7
Compressed hours of working (working longer, but fewer days)	58.9
Childcare vouchers or subsidy	56.5
Job-share	54.6
Paid career break	53.7
Time off for emergencies within the family (unpaid)	51.1
Working at home	48.6
Company car	48.4
Retail vouchers	48.3
Unpaid career break	47.8
School term-time only contracts	46.8
Paternity leave (unpaid)	44.8

A6.4: The relationship between gender, occupational level, caring responsibilities and conflict, and current and intended use of flexible working practices

Flexible working measure Predictor variables	Current	Intended
Age	0.00	−0.07**
Gender	−0.05	0.08**
Managerial level	0.12***	0.13***
Semi-skilled level	−0.04	−0.04
Caring responsibilities	0.02	0.04
Work–family conflict	−0.10***	0.06*
Family–work conflict	0.17***	0.01
Family–work support	0.05	0.09***
Hours worked	−0.02	−0.04
R^2	0.05***	0.05***

Note: Non-italicised figures are standardised regression coefficients. Italicised figures are total variance accounted for.
* $p<0.05$, ** $p<0.01$, *** $p<0.001$.

A6.5: Hours worked, stress (GHQ), sickness and turnover intention – analysis of variance statistics showing effects as a function of gender, occupational level and caring responsibilities (with age covaried)

	Univariate F statistics (1,650df)			
	Hours worked	GHQ score	Days of sickness (log-transformed)	Turnover intention
Age (covariate)	0.39	0.10	0.10	22.01*** (−)
Gender	21.71***	1.48	28.47***	0.06
Level	4.71**	36.99***	15.08***	0.70
Carer	0.05	7.97**	1.60	0.71
Gender x Level	1.53	12.41***	0.45	0.18
Gender x Carer	0.06	0.49	7.32**	0.01
Level x Carer	0.26	0.03	1.38	1.31
Gender x Level x Carer	0.76	0.76	0.51	1.14

Note: * $p<0.05$, ** $p<0.01$, *** $p<0.001$. Where the effect of age is significant, the direction of the relationship is shown in brackets. + indicates that scores on the item become higher with increasing age, − indicates that scores on the item become lower with increasing age.

Chapter 7

A7.1: Multivariate ANOVA statistics for the effects of age, gender, occupational level and caring responsibilities on workplace culture measures

	Univariate *F* statistics (1,650df)				Multivariate *F*
	Managerial support	Negative career consequences	Organisational time demands	Union support for family-friendly policies	
Age (covariate)	1.27	8.16** (+)	9.86** (+)	10.68*** (+)	5.93***
Gender	0.59	0.35	8.54**	5.67*	4.38**
Level	19.19***	3.71*	7.72***	2.86	14.25***
Carer	1.52	2.40	3.01	0.52	0.96
Gender x Level	0.45	0.46	1.09	0.26	0.97
Gender x Carer	0.64	3.16	1.31	4.25*	2.19
Level x Carer	2.05	0.93	0.19	0.98	1.64
Gender x Level x Carer	1.27	1.33	0.21	0.32	0.84

Note: Listwise deletion was used for missing data; that is, data were only included in this analysis for participants who completed all four items. * $p<0.05$, ** $p<0.01$, *** $p<0.001$. Where the effect of age is significant, the direction of the relationship is shown in brackets. + indicates that scores on the item become higher with increasing age, – indicates that scores on the item become lower with increasing age.

A7.2a: Means (and standard deviations) as a function of gender, occupational level and caring responsibilities

	Men (n=1,109)	Women (n=584)	Managerial (n=544)	Skilled (n=798)	Semi-skilled (n=344)	Non-carer (n=1,023)	Carer (n=677)	Overall mean
Management support	4.06 (1.02)	4.00 (1.15)	4.25 (0.92)	4.03 (1.09)	3.75 (1.17)	4.06 (1.08)	4.02 (1.05)	4.03 (1.07)
Negative career consequences	3.84 (1.09)	3.72 (1.31)	3.98 (1.07)	3.70 (1.17)	3.73 (1.29)	3.76 (1.20)	3.86 (1.13)	3.85 (1.16)
Organisational demands	4.11 (1.46)	3.71 (1.49)	4.20 (1.45)	3.89 (1.52)	3.78 (1.42)	3.89 (1.48)	4.08 (1.48)	3.98 (1.48)
Union support for family-friendly practices	4.27 (1.28)	4.40 (1.47)	4.21 (1.11)	4.41 (1.41)	4.31 (1.50)	4.36 (1.37)	4.26 (1.31)	4.32 (1.35)

Note: Scores for all variables may range from 1 to 7, where 7 represents stronger agreement.

A7.2b: Percentage agreeing (over 4 on a 7-point scale ranging from 1 = strongly disagree to 7 = strongly agree) with workplace culture measures, as a function of gender, occupational level and caring responsibilities

	Men (n=1,109)	Women (n=584)	Managerial (n=544)	Skilled (n=798)	Semi-skilled (n=344)	Non-carer (n=1,023)	Carer (n=677)	Overall %
Management support	54.5	50.9	62.2	52.5	41.3***	53.7	52.4	53.3
Negative career consequences	41.1	38.6	46.4	37.0	36.9***	38.6	42.6	40.2
Organisational demands	50.9	37.6***	52.8	44.2	39.8***	43.7	49.9	46.3
Union support for family-friendly practices	55.2	57.3	53.2	58.0	55.6	56.7	54.9	55.9

Note: Asterisks indicate significant differences in percentages between comparable groups (that is, gender difference, occupation difference or caring difference). * $p<0.05$, ** $p<0.01$, *** $p<0.001$ by chi square statistics.

Chapter 8

A8.1: Regression statistics for relationships between attitudes and health and turnover intention

Outcomes *Predictor variables*	Stress	Days of sickness	Turnover intention
Step 1			
Age	0.01	−0.01	−0.12***
Gender	−0.01	0.14***	0.01
Managerial level	0.33***	−0.15***	0.03
Semi-skilled level	0.02	0.03	0.01
Care responsibilities	0.07**	0.03	−0.02
Step 1 R²	*0.11****	0.06***	0.02***
Step 2			
Age	0.01	−0.01	−0.12***
Gender	−0.01	0.12***	0.01
Managerial level	0.33***	−0.16***	0.05
Semi-skilled level	0.02	0.03	0.01
Care responsibilities	0.07**	0.03	−0.03
Personal benefits	0.06*	0.06*	0.01
Employer benefits	0.04	−0.02	−0.02
Employee success	−0.08***	−0.03	−0.03
Engagement	−0.02	0.02	0.04
Poorer performance	0.10***	−0.04	0.02
Long hours negative	0.05	00.01	−0.10***
Long hours positive	0.05	0.06*	0.10***
Total R²	*0.13****	*0.07****	*0.04****

Note: Asterisks indicate significant differences in percentages between comparable groups (that is, gender difference, occupation difference or caring difference). * $p<0.05$, ** $p<0.01$, *** $p<0.001$ by chi square statistics.

Appendix B:
Changes in statutory rights

Our questionnaire survey was conducted prior to the changes in statutory rights for parents which came into effect in April 2003. Table B.1 summarises the current employment rights for people with children.

B.1: Statutory rights in 2002 and changes for 2003

	The position in 2002	Change from April 2003
Ordinary maternity leave (OML) and Statutory Maternity Pay (SMP)	18 weeks	26 weeks
Additional maternity leave (AML)	For women with one year's service by the 11th week before the expected week of childbirth (EWC). Starts at the end of OML and lasts for 29 weeks from the birth. The maximum leave entitlement is 11 weeks before the EWC and 29 weeks from the birth	For women with 26 weeks' service by the 15th week before the EWC (same service condition as for SMP). Lasts for 26 weeks from the end of OML. The maximum leave entitlement is therefore 52 weeks
Statutory Maternity Pay	For those who qualify: 6 weeks at 90% of pay and £75 per week for 12 weeks. 18 weeks in all	For those who qualify: 6 weeks at 90% of pay and £100 per week for 20 weeks. 26 weeks in all
Parental leave	From Jan 2002, the right to up to 13 weeks' unpaid leave for each child and more for disabled children. Different qualifying dates, see: http://www.dti.gov.uk/er/intguid1.htm	Unchanged
Paternity leave	May take unpaid parental leave around the time of the birth	A right to two weeks' paid paternity leave at £100 a week
Adoption leave	May take unpaid parental leave around the time of the adoption	26 weeks' paid adoption leave at £100 a week; a further 26 weeks' unpaid leave
Flexible hours	No statutory rights	A right for those with children under 6, or disabled children under 18, to request flexible working hours